Yōko Kanno's Cowboy Bebop Soundtrack

33 1/3 Global

33 1/3 Global, a series related to but independent from **33 1/3**, takes the format of the original series of short, music-based books and brings the focus to music throughout the world. With initial volumes focusing on Japanese and Brazilian music, the series will also include volumes on the popular music of Australia/Oceania, Europe, Africa, the Middle East, and more.

33 1/3 Japan

Series Editor: Noriko Manabe
Series Board: Mariē Abe, Michael Bourdaghs, Shelley Brunt, Kevin Fellezs, Akitsugu Kawamoto, Yoshitaka Mōri, Dexter Thomas, Christine Yano
Spanning a range of artists and genres—from the 1960s rock of Happy End to technopop band Yellow Magic Orchestra, the Shibuya-kei of Cornelius, classic anime series *Cowboy Bebop*, J-Pop/EDM hybrid Perfume, and vocaloid star Hatsune Miku—**33 1/3 Japan** is a series devoted to in-depth examination of Japanese music of the twentieth and twenty-first centuries.

Published Titles:
Supercell's *Supercell* by Keisuke Yamada
Forthcoming titles:
Perfume's *Game* by Patrick St. Michel

33 1/3 Brazil

Series Editor: Jason Stanyek
Covering the genres of samba, tropicália, rock, hip hop, forró, bossa nova, heavy metal, and funk, among others, **33 1/3 Brazil** is a series devoted to in-depth examination of the most important Brazilian albums of the twentieth and twenty-first centuries.

Published Titles:
Caetano Veloso's *A Foreign Sound* by Barbara Browning
Forthcoming titles:
Tim Maia's *Tim Maia Racional Vols. 1 & 2* by Allen Thayer
João Gilberto and Stan Getz's *Getz/Gilberto* by Brian McCann

Yōko Kanno's Cowboy Bebop Soundtrack

Rose Bridges

Noriko Manabe, Series Editor

Bloomsbury Academic
An imprint of Bloomsbury Publishing Inc.

BLOOMSBURY

NEW YORK • LONDON • OXFORD • NEW DELHI • SYDNEY

Bloomsbury Academic
An imprint of Bloomsbury Publishing Inc.

50 Bedford Square	1385 Broadway
London	New York
WC1B 3DP	NY 10018
UK	USA

www.bloomsbury.com

First published 2017

Library of Congress Cataloging-in-Publication Data
Names: Bridges, Rose author.
Title: Yoko Kanno's Cowboy bebop soundtrack / Rose Bridges.
Description: New York, NY : Bloomsbury Academic, 2017. | Series: 33 1/3 Japan | Includes bibliographical references and index.
Identifiers: LCCN 2017020563 (print) | LCCN 2017021212 (ebook) | ISBN 9781501325861 (ePDF) | ISBN 9781501325878 (ePUB) | ISBN 9781501325847 (hardcover : alk. paper)
Subjects: LCSH: Kanno, Yoko–Criticism and interpretation. | Animated television music--Japan--History and criticism. | Cowboy bebop (Animated television program)
Classification: LCC ML410.K166 (ebook) | LCC ML410.K166 B75 2017 (print) | DDC 781.5/46092--dc23
LC record available at https://lccn.loc.gov/2017020563

ISBN: HB: 978-1-5013-2584-7
PB: 978-1-5013-2585-4
ePub: 978-1-5013-2587-8
ePDF: 978-1-5013-2586-1

Series: 33⅓ Japan

Cover image © pikepicture/Shutterstock

Typeset in the U.K. by Fakenham Prepress Solutions, Fakenham, Norfolk NR21 8NN

To find out more about our authors and books visit www.bloomsbury.com. Here you will find extracts, author interviews, details of forthcoming events and the option to sign up for our newsletters.

Contents

Acknowledgments

I want to thank everyone who played a role in helping make this book possible. This includes my editor, Noriko Manabe, who also graciously helped me procure interviews and conducted them on my behalf in Japan; my advisors at the University of Texas, including Hannah Lewis, James Buhler, and Charles Carson; and Josh Goring of Strawberry Hill Music, for his assistance in setting up interviews with North American musicians from the *Cowboy Bebop* soundtrack.

I also want to thank everyone who agreed to interviews with me for this book: Emily Bindiger, Steve Blum, Steve Conte, Scott Matthew, Mary McGlynn, Raj Ramayya, and last, but not least, Yōko Kanno and Shinichirō Watanabe. This book would not be possible without your insights and eagerness to help.

I want to thank my father, Dan Bridges, for giving me so much of the early musical education in classic rock-and-roll that made me the musicologist I am today. I want to thank the teacher, Carol Rexer, who first nurtured in me the dream of writing a book one day, a dream I have finally achieved. Last, but not least, I want to thank my mother and stepfather, Karen and Randy Cullen, for their supportiveness as I've dedicated the past two years of my life to this book. I also thank my mother for passing on her love of movies to me, which has guided my studies of film music.

Note on Japanese Names and English Dubs

Japanese names are usually presented as family name first, followed by given name. However, as a large base of Western anime fans is already familiar with the names of *Cowboy Bebop* producer Shinichirō WATANABE, composer Yōko KANNO, and other artists in Western format, all Japanese names are presented as given name first, family name last.

Quotations of dialogue have been taken from the English dub of *Cowboy Bebop*, as it is familiar to the English-language fanbase. The author compared the dub against the English subtitles on the Japanese version to check the accuracy of the translation.

Introduction: *3, 2, 1 . . . Let's Jam!*

Almost every episode of the space-western anime series *Cowboy Bebop* opens with the same music: its exuberant, jazzy theme song, "Tank!" After a blast of rapid brass chords, a walking bass line snakes across the musical texture as a male voice intones, "I think it's time we blow this scene, get everybody and the stuff together. Okay, 3, 2, 1, let's jam!" On screen, a silhouette of main character Spike Spiegel lights a cigarette. Immediately after, the descending, staccato main theme appears in saxophones, and Spike takes off running. The music continues to introduce other jazzy themes, against silhouettes of characters and their spaceships moving against solid, primary color backgrounds. In the interview for the book, Kanno described it as originally written to be "one of the background-music tracks, but Director Watanabe chose to use it as the opening theme . . . I only recorded about two takes of it, so the mistakes and small flaws are still in the track. But that vigorousness was in the spirit of brass bands, and I thought that was good" (Yōko Kanno, email communication with Noriko Manabe, December 4, 2016; translation by Manabe).

In spite of Kanno's original intentions, "Tank!" defines the show for viewers because of its status as the theme song for the series. It promises a fast-paced, action-filled, and above all cool experience. The question for viewers is, how much—and how consistently—does *Cowboy Bebop* live up to these promises?

Like many people of my generation, I grew up with anime. I watched *Sailor Moon*, *Pokémon*, and *Digimon* on TV as a child, and was in high school during the mid-2000s anime boom, when anime and manga were a relatively mainstream part of nerd culture. While I enjoyed a few series, I never really took to anime as a medium until college, when a friend reintroduced me with the series *Puella Magi Madoka Magica* (2011). Yuki Kajiura's soundtrack blew me away, and I was eager to check out more anime that had amazing music. This naturally led me to *Cowboy Bebop*.

Even before I heard a note of it, *Cowboy Bebop* seemed designed to speak to me, with its episode (or "session") titles from my favorite classic rock songs. The actual music, though, was some of the most incredible I'd ever heard in film media. Individual scenes in *Cowboy Bebop* shed light on the importance of music in audiovisual storytelling. More than any other anime series, *Cowboy Bebop* made me want to study film music as a musicologist. This series has had a profound influence on my own life and journeys as a musicologist and composer.

Why does *Cowboy Bebop* need a guide? Why can't we just "sit back, relax and enjoy the show," as one of Watanabe's other anime, *Samurai Champloo*, implores its viewers? Because *Cowboy Bebop* is much deeper than it looks at first glance, full of thoughtful statements about human nature and, on a more metatextual level, the nature of artistic genre. One of *Cowboy Bebop*'s most contemplative elements is its music, which has a close relationship to the narrative and visual elements of the series. Watanabe made it clear in the interview for this book that the music often influenced the story (rather than the other way around), and so music is essential to enjoying *Cowboy Bebop*.

I am not alone in my opinions about *Cowboy Bebop*: Kanno's soundtrack is one of the most celebrated in the medium, regularly included on lists of the best anime music—usually at the top. I know there are many people who enjoy this soundtrack, but who may not have the specific knowledge of music, film theory, and/or anime to fully appreciate why the music is the way it is, or its role in shaping the series. I hope that my guide can help them with that, toward a more informed enjoyment of one of the best that anime has to offer.

1 "The Work Which Becomes a New Genre Itself": Shinichirō Watanabe's Influences and Legacy

Referenced External Works
Dirty Harry (1971)
Samurai Champloo (2004–5)
Kids on the Slope (2012)
Space Dandy (2014)

Studying film music requires reflecting on a complex web of influences and voices. This is especially true with anime, as so many are produced by committee. These multiple voices are essential for understanding what makes *Cowboy Bebop*, and its music, so special among the anime canon. None the less, this book has Yōko Kanno's name in the title, as the composer of the *Cowboy Bebop* soundtrack. A similar pattern is seen in the titles of books in the 33 1/3 series, including the other pre-existing soundtrack book, Andrew Schartmann's *Koji Kondo's Super Mario Bros. Soundtrack*. Most importantly,

Yōko Kanno has a strong compositional voice that should be reflected in the title of the book.

That being said, much of film music's effectiveness lies in its use in specific moments. Therefore, one cannot discount the influence of the director over the music of a film or TV series. Few directors follow this approach so much as Shinichirō Watanabe, the director of the *Cowboy Bebop* series and movie. Watanabe has a reputation for anime where music closely interacts with the series content. Kanno frequently collaborates with Watanabe, but even in his soundtracks without her, there are similarly strong relationships between music and anime. In my interviews with Mary McGlynn, the Automated Dialogue Replacement (ADR) director for the *Cowboy Bebop* English dub and the voice of Julia, and Steve Blum, the voice of Spike Spiegel, they described how the music plays an integral role in telling the story. "The way Watanabe sculpted the series," McGlynn said, "this show breathed. There's storytelling through music, as well as through animation and through dialogue. But that didn't happen all at the same time ... The music is one of the strongest voices in the show" (Steve Blum and Mary McGlynn, Skype interview with the author, July 17, 2016).

In an email exchange that Noriko Manabe (the 33 1/3 Japan series editor) and I conducted, Yōko Kanno gave a vivid description of Watanabe's relationship with music in his series:

> There is no other director who treats musical choices as his own self-expression like Watanabe does. It's like that delicate and earnest feeling of when you're a junior high school student, and you give your favorite music to someone of the opposite sex so that they would understand you ... He has an abundance of knowledge ... His treatment of music is very

considered, and I feel he respects musicians. Sometimes he even seems to value the music over the story. (Kanno, email communication)

In the interview Manabe conducted for this book in Japan in July 2016, Watanabe discussed the way the series was created, its influences, and its similarities and differences from his other work. This chapter draws on this interview to explain the origins of *Cowboy Bebop*, Watanabe's influences for the use of music in this series, and to place *Cowboy Bebop* within the context of Watanabe's oeuvre.

The Birth of *Cowboy Bebop*

Watanabe considers *Cowboy Bebop*'s production as different from typical anime production. Originally, he wanted to name it "Nagareboshi," or "Falling Star," after a song by Shibuya-*kei* star Kenji Ozawa (the nephew of Boston Symphony conductor Seiji Ozawa), but it ran foul of copyright laws in Japan.[1] So, instead, he came up with the title *Cowboy Bebop* to describe two of the important reference points of the series: cowboy-western films (especially those that centered on bounty hunters like the show's main character, Spike) and jazz.

The text in the opening titles describes the creation of the bebop genre in the 1940s and its improvisatory, artistic nature compared to earlier forms of jazz. In Watanabe's discussion of the production details, it is clear that this description extends to the way that the series was made: "The staff (for *Cowboy Bebop*) were also like bebop musicians. We didn't want to make anime in a pattern that was already set. So I gave it that title" (Shinichirō Watanabe, interview with Noriko Manabe, Tokyo,

July 8, 2016; translation by Manabe. Hereafter "Watanabe, interview"). Many aspects of anime production that are usually decided well in advance of the series were created or decided on the fly. This included much of the music.

To understand the music of the series, it is worth explaining some important information about typical anime TV series production.[2] While some aspects of anime series are planned in advance, the actual episodes—the visual production—are completed week-by-week while the series is airing. (This is unlike American television production, especially in the current era of "prestige TV," in which series are usually completed far ahead of the airdate.) Because composing, finding musicians for, and recording all the music takes much longer than that schedule allows, anime creators must solicit composers and order music from them well in advance of the rest of the anime's production. This allows anime to often create the visuals to fit the music for that scene, instead of the other way around. Music orders can be specific and include certain musical styles, instrumentations, etc. that they desire, or just a request for music based on the specific scene or emotion.

Watanabe said that about half of the soundtrack was ordered that way. The other half came from what Watanabe called "free sessions"—created later like the rest of the series. Because this improvisatory approach characterized the production of the series, he referred to the episodes as "sessions," indicating their affinities with improvisatory jazz performances. Watanabe wanted the "bebop" moniker to indicate how independent and free the characters were, and how their actions were "improvisatory" (Watanabe, interview). The anime's production process mirrored this ethos.

I interviewed several musicians who worked with Yōko Kanno on the soundtrack of the *Cowboy Bebop* series and movie: Emily Bindiger, Steve Conte, Scott Matthew, and Raj Ramayya. All of them confirmed that they did not know anything about the series going into the project, only what Kanno wanted them to do musically. That reveals just how early in the production process music can be composed for anime—including this series. As explained further in this and other chapters, this meant that music could have a measurable effect on the anime's visuals and story.

Watanabe's Film-Musical Influences

In the interview for the book, Watanabe mentioned some of his influences on the music in the film. While many articles on *Cowboy Bebop* mention the influence of John Woo's action films and the *Lupin III* anime franchise, Watanabe actually denied that *Lupin III* was an influence, saying it was low down on his list of influences and that he was primarily interested in the first series. He also said Woo's films mostly influenced other aspects of production, not music or sound. Instead, Watanabe cited the films of Sam Peckinpah—known for revisionist westerns such as *The Wild Bunch* (1969) and *Pat Garrett and Billy the Kid* (1973), the latter of which is possibly best known for its soundtrack by Bob Dylan. The title of Dylan's biggest hit from the soundtrack, "Knockin' on Heaven's Door," was used for the name of the *Cowboy Bebop* feature film.

Despite that textual connection between *Pat Garrett and Billy the Kid* and *Cowboy Bebop*, I had trouble finding any direct connections between either of those Peckinpah soundtracks and the *Cowboy Bebop* soundtrack. There was a stronger connection with the other major Hollywood film Watanabe suggested as a musical influence: *Dirty Harry*

(1971). He even referred to the prolific Don Siegel as just "the *Dirty Harry* director" (Watanabe, interview). There are broader genre similarities between the two works, such as their heavy reliance on the aesthetics of *film noir*, the popular genre of urban pulp and crime films from the 1940s (the same decade when bebop emerged). Yvonne Tasker discusses how *Dirty Harry* creates a 1970s version of the "*noir* city," mainly through "its equation of dark urban spaces with dubious morality" (2015: 111–12). *Cowboy Bebop* does the same, although it retains more affection for the urban lifestyle, making it seem glamorous and inviting as well as dangerous. There are more similarities in the music of the two works, mainly the audiovisual connections and the use of genres such as jazz. Lalo Schifrin's score for *Dirty Harry* often blends genres; a fast-paced jazz number turns into a slow, trippy, ethereal psychedelic rock or ambient track in a matter of seconds. This blend is comparable to *Cowboy Bebop*'s use of musical genre, where music travels across genre boundaries over the course of one track. Consider, for example, the full version of "Space Lion" that takes up the last seven minutes of session 13, "Jupiter Jazz (Part 2)," as it evolves from a jazz saxophone solo into a soft rock ballad.

Dirty Harry's music supports its visuals in interesting and surprising ways. It often couples a camera going out of focus with increasingly experimental psychedelic music, as though both the visual and aural lenses are getting "hazy." It also uses audiovisual counterpoint, where the music does not match the mood of the scene. This is particularly true of the final sequence involving a mass kidnapping by Scorpio, a serial killer and the film's primary villain. The child victims' insistent singing of nursery rhyme tunes is juxtaposed against their threatening situation—Scorpio using them as hostages—even before the children are fully aware of their plight. The juxtaposition of innocence with horror makes the latter more disturbing; it is a reminder of just how twisted Scorpio is. *Cowboy Bebop* takes audiovisual counterpoint further, actually adding tenderness to tense scenes, such as the choral, lullaby-like melody of "Green Bird" as Spike falls from a church. It creates a true mixture of moods, rather than merely enhancing one of them through contrast.

Both works also use jazz to enhance the feeling of the *noir* city, including in action sequences. *Dirty Harry* features what might be called acid jazz in chase and search scenes. It usually blends into another style quickly, and the effect is that the music sounds sleazy, adding to the decadence of the urban environment. The big-band jazz used in *Cowboy Bebop*'s action sequences instead emphasizes the coolness and fun of the situation. It shows off Spike's abilities as a brisk, fun action hero without bringing down the other characters and environment around him.

It is easy to hear how *Dirty Harry*'s groundbreaking score, which was ahead of its time in combining genres such as jazz and psychedelic rock, influenced *Cowboy Bebop*. I would argue, though, that *Cowboy Bebop* took these techniques even further, and in a more playful, less cynical direction.

There is one place where *Cowboy Bebop* more closely follows *Dirty Harry*'s musical patterns, particularly its use of abrupt dissonant chords with sparse melodies for horror. That is in session 20, "Pierrot le Fou," discussed here in Chapter 4.

The Watanabe Filmography and Style: A Brief Tour

By placing *Cowboy Bebop* within the context of Watanabe's other output, we can better understand his handling of music. Prior to *Bebop*, he worked as a co-director on *Macross Plus* (1994), but Watanabe made it clear that he did not have complete control over the music: "I didn't always like the songs [the music producer and Shōji Kawamori, the other co-director] were choosing, but I was often outvoted by the other two. I still think the songs I picked were better. I learned from that experience that you have to pick the music yourself" (Watanabe, interview). *Cowboy Bebop* was the series that gave Watanabe the clout to do what he wanted with his future series, including music.

The first of his series following *Bebop* was *Samurai Champloo*, a 2004–5 series Watanabe directed, with animation production by the defunct anime studio Manglobe. *Samurai Champloo* is ostensibly a *chanbara* (samurai) series, but breaks from the genre's conventions.[3] The series presents a gleefully anachronistic portrait of its Edo period (1603–1868) setting, with the first episode making visual comparisons to modern street-gang culture. It blends its period features from a time when Japan was cut off from the rest of the world with the trappings of modern Western popular culture.[4]

The soundtrack reflects this in its use of hip-hop. Various Japanese hip hop DJs, including Nujabes, and DJ Tsutschie of the Japanese rap group Shakkazombie contributed to the hip-hop soundtrack (Watanabe did not approach Kanno because of her lack of familiarity with the genre).[5] Much of *Samurai Champloo*'s hip-hop is instrumental, and, as with many early hip-hop DJ tracks, they range from R&B to funk, even to jazz. What makes them identifiable as hip-hop is both the use of rapping in the opening theme and the visual components of the series: protagonist Mugen's anachronistic, modern urban appearance, graffiti art in the opening sequence, and the fight choreography that resembles breakdancing. *Samurai Champloo* also announces scene changes with "record scratch" sound effects, resembling the way that hip-hop producers and DJs use electronic remixing to repeat certain syllables. Both the sound and visuals suggest repetition, adding to the anachronistic atmosphere of the series, as though the recording technology existed in this pre-recording world. *Samurai Champloo* features all of what Tricia Rose defines as the "four elements of hip hop": graffiti, breakdancing, DJs, and MCs (1999: 191–221).

Watanabe stressed in the Manabe interview that all his series were different: "My concerns are not to repeat what we have done before. We won't do another *Bebop*. We would make a totally different thing" (Watanabe, interview). Still, it's hard not to read *Samurai Champloo* as building on the *Cowboy Bebop*'s musical innovations. *Champloo* stretches the relationship between music, visuals, and narrative to its limit. It brings its hip-hop soundtrack even further into the story, directly affecting the world it creates.

Watanabe's next directorial effort was in 2012, with the manga adaptation *Kids on the Slope*. The story follows a group of Japanese teenagers in the 1960s as they bond over playing and listening to jazz. Much of the music in the series is diegetic (i.e., existing in the world of the series); it is the music of characters performing and listening to records. Consequently, most of the music is pre-existing. The characters bond to the sounds of a variety of jazz artists who were popular in Japan at the time, most notably Art Blakey, whose song "Moanin'" repeats throughout the series.[6] The use of "Moanin'" shows that *Kids on the Slope* employs pre-existing music even in non-diegetic ways (i.e., existing only for the viewer, not within the world of the show), creating less of a need for an original score compared to Watanabe's previous anime. There are still many original works by Yōko Kanno in the non-diegetic background music. Her score includes both jazz and more traditional orchestral scoring, to set it apart from the music the characters listen to and play in the series. *Kids on the Slope* is a much more traditional use of music than Watanabe's previous soundtracks, though it still reflects Watanabe's own passion for jazz from a young age.

Of Shinichirō Watanabe's two 2014 works, *Space Dandy* and *Terror in Resonance*, the former is more relevant to this discussion. *Space Dandy* takes the episodic elements of *Cowboy Bebop* and *Samurai Champloo* even further. The series has different directors, writers, and composers for every episode, as well as negative continuity similar to many American adult animation series, like those that aired alongside Watanabe's series on Adult Swim.[7] This reflects the fact that it was developed specifically to air concurrently in Japan and the United States, with heavy collaboration from the American anime licensing company Funimation. Watanabe also used the series to promote the creative output of other anime directors. Contributors include Watanabe's protégées and collaborators like director Sayo Yamamoto and *Bebop* screenwriter Keiko Nobumoto, and other influential voices in anime like Masaki Yuasa.[8]

This resulted in a varied musical landscape that adjusts to fit the many different genres that *Dandy*'s various creators moved through: the musical, zombie parody, sports flick, and post-modern sci-fi. While *Space Dandy* can be considered an entry in the Watanabe–Kanno filmography, as Kanno wrote music for it (including the ending theme, "Welcome to the X Dimension"), she is just one of many composers Watanabe worked with on the series. "I worked with a lot of musicians: twenty artists/groups participated," Watanabe said in the Manabe interview. "I gave them directions in different ways."

Despite the many musical voices involved, there are still distinct musical patterns across *Space Dandy*. The main character, Dandy, sports a pompadour, flashy suits, and uses exaggerated dance movements reminiscent of the disco era. The musical landscape reflects this; it includes funk, disco, and other retro genres, especially "kitschy" ones like surf music, and "1980s pop" (according to Watanabe in the interview). Both the Kanno-composed ending theme and the opening theme, "Viva Namida," are disco-inspired, based on their use of instruments (particularly brass timbres and synthesizer) and Dandy's eccentric dance moves in the visuals.

Terror in Resonance is more of a departure for Watanabe in terms of plot and themes. It is a more serious work than others and focuses on deeper, more fraught issues, like terrorism, Japanese nationalism, American neo-imperialism, and child abuse. However, visually and sonically *Terror in Resonance* is, like other Watanabe–Kanno collaborations, an outstanding spectacle. Much of the music was recorded in Iceland, and reflects the influences of Icelandic musicians such as Björk and Sigur Rós, as well as the "harsh landscape," according to Kanno (Tomita 2014). *Terror in Resonance* is one of Kanno's most eclectic scores, and later in the book I discuss it briefly in the context of her larger career.

Watanabe also worked as a music producer on two of protégée Sayo Yamamoto's solo directorial efforts, *Michiko & Hatchin* (2008–9) and *Lupin III: The Woman Called Fujiko Mine* (2012).[9] *Michiko & Hatchin* is set in Brazil and includes a soundtrack by Brazilian musician Alexandre Kassin, and is full of native Brazilian music genres like samba. *The Woman Called Fujiko Mine* is a prequel to the original *Lupin III* series from 1971–2. The prequel takes place in the 1960s and includes a soundtrack that features the era's modern, experimental jazz. Both soundtracks have a very free, improvisatory atmosphere, reflecting the focus in both series on free-spirited women (the titular Michiko and Fujiko) struggling against society. While Watanabe, as music producer rather than director or composer, is not necessarily the primary "musical voice" for those series (especially since Yamamoto herself is another distinctive, "auteur" director), it is interesting how these series exhibit his tendencies toward music that interacts with and reflects the narrative world. Both soundtracks seem as if they evolved from the "free sessions" Watanabe discusses throughout interviews about *Cowboy Bebop*.

Examining Watanabe's body of work puts *Cowboy Bebop* in the stylistic context necessary to understand this soundtrack and its distinctiveness from other anime soundtracks. *Cowboy Bebop* is special, not least because of the strong authorial voices of its creative collaborators, like Watanabe and Kanno. The next chapter discusses Yōko Kanno's musical influences and the place of the *Cowboy Bebop* soundtrack in her larger body of work.

2 Mish-Mash Blues: Analyzing Yōko Kanno's Style

Referenced External Works
Macross Plus (1994)
Wolf's Rain (2003)

Yōko Kanno's music is difficult to categorize. Throughout my interviews with various musicians who worked on *Cowboy Bebop*, the word that came up over and over to describe Kanno's music was "eclectic." She explores all over the musical map to find a sound that fits the unique world of the series. Steve Conte, who sang vocals on "Call Me Call Me," the album version of "Rain," and other tracks, described Kanno as a "total chameleon … which I love, because I am, too" (Steve Conte, Skype interview with the author, May 10, 2016). Though this aspect makes her scores more interesting, it also makes it difficult to approach the topic of this chapter: what does a score by Yōko Kanno sound like? Can her style even be narrowed down to a single paradigm?

It is a common question when dealing with film music. Many film composers have distinctive musical thumbprints, ones they carry throughout their scores even with slight adaptations to fit each film. Anime is no exception to that rule; many of the medium's celebrated composers, from Yuki Kajiura (*.hack//SIGN*, *Madoka Magica*, *Sword Art Online*) to Hiroyuki Sawano (*Attack on Titan*, *Kill la Kill*) write music which fans easily recognize within seconds. Yōko Kanno does not fit into that mold. While there are certainly stylistic comparisons one can make with individual tracks across her works, there is no one "Yōko Kanno sound."

That is not to say that Kanno does not have stylistic preoccupations. In the interview, Raj Ramayya, a vocalist and ghostwriter who worked with Kanno from her days scoring commercials to *Cowboy Bebop* and *Wolf's Rain*, described her tastes as "influenced very heavily by American pop and rock. She would send us reference songs from Beck and Foo Fighters. That's why her music resonates so well with Americans … She's an American rock person" (Raj Ramayya, Skype interview with the author, April 29, 2016). When I asked him what he brought to the soundtrack, he cited that same "British or American sound," theorizing that Kanno selected him and other musicians based on that sound. "[I was chosen] because of the Beatlesque kind of thing [Ramayya also worked on Japanese commercials as the voice of John Lennon], and Steve [Conte] because of American hard rock, blues-rock" (Ramayya, interview).

Kanno stated she did not pick musicians based on these specifications, but definitely had them in mind when writing their music. "Usually, I have a set of performers, and I compose to fit those people. [Otherwise,] I suspect you wouldn't get great results … I always would like to meet with musicians without preconceptions. If the person is unexpectedly a classical performer or heavy metal drummer, a singer of school-chorus songs or *minyō* (traditional folk) songs, I like making music that suits that person or that I want them to perform. It's the same as when a scriptwriter writes with the actor in mind" (Kanno, email communication).

Still, those genres do not show up on all of her soundtracks, which is why I call them "preoccupations." Kanno also stresses in interviews that she does not try to go for any particular sound; in her response for this book, she even said that she doesn't "listen to music while classifying it by genre." Instead of describing music by era, level of technique, or affect, she described her musical influences as "the sounds of birds, the waves, or cars. A large variety of sounds reach my ears and affect me, consciously and unconsciously."

I argue that Kanno has a style, and it actually lies in her eclecticism.[1] Kanno finds ways to combine different genres not only across soundtrack albums, but within individual musical tracks in her work. Her own comments seem to support this, as she describes her music as "omnivorous. Because I often get requests for both grand and delicate pieces, I think my music is understood as having both orientations" (Kanno, email communication).

Additionally, Kanno is uniquely skilled at creating a consistent musical landscape for her series, creating music that sets the scene and seems like it could exist in the story's world. This scene-setting is particularly pronounced in her collaborations with Watanabe, as he takes a similar approach to music in film, but it carries through even with Kanno's work with other directors. This consistency seems to be the product of sheer inspiration, as Kanno does not limit herself to the music she had been directed to write. As Watanabe commented, "Kanno would get inspired and produce songs I didn't ask for. She'd say, this kind of image came to mind, so I produced this. There are dozens of [unsolicited] songs like this. And the unusual songs inspired me, and I would build scenes around them" (Watanabe, interview). Kanno confirmed this process: "Rather than composing music for this-and-that kind of scene, I more often present all the music I felt about the work [anime] without limitations, and the director chooses the music he wants. For that reason, my music relates to the work from a very early stage, and I think that is probably a special feature of my soundtracks" (Kanno, email communication).

Kanno specified that she was not as focused in *Cowboy Bebop* on building a larger musical world: "In my previous work, I had worked so hard to create the background scene and culture of a work from complete scratch, and I had gotten tired of thinking through the logic behind it" (Kanno, email communication). Still, she gave examples of music she wrote for *Cowboy Bebop* that was inspired by particular places. For example, "Car 24" came from a trip to New York: "I felt I must go right now to see the sights, so I rented a taxi for a few hours. That taxi company was named Car 24 ... The New York that I saw then became that song" (Kanno, email communication).

To give a broader sense of Kanno's career and how the *Cowboy Bebop* soundtrack fits into it, this chapter examines some of her notable anime scores, including those both with and without Watanabe. Kanno's resume is long, including some of the biggest franchises in anime (such as *Macross* and *Gundam*), and so an in-depth analysis is beyond the scope of this book. None the less, analyzing a few noteworthy scores will help to put her *Cowboy Bebop* score in the context of her larger career. Particular attention will be given to *Macross Plus* and *Wolf's Rain*, which share writing and, in the former's case, directing staff with *Cowboy Bebop*. The soundtracks also parallel *Bebop*'s, in that they include genre fusion and manipulation.

Musical Background and Early Career

One of Kanno's few printed interviews in English is from 2014 (around the time of the release of her soundtrack for *Terror in Resonance*) by the Japanese musician and music producer Akihiro Tomita for the Red Bull Music Academy website. In the interview, Kanno gives some clues to her upbringing and musical background, and to the diverse influences on her more notable anime soundtracks.

In English language interviews, Kanno claims to have taught herself the piano intuitively as a child: "There was a piano at my house and I said 'What is this?' I simply played when I felt like it and made original music" (Tomita 2014). According to a July 2009 interview in Japan's *Music Magazine*, Kanno attended group piano classes as a young child, but she found these classes to be restrictive and quit (Takahashi 2009).

Kanno attended a Catholic kindergarten, where she played the organ; in the English-language interviews, she describes this experience as an important part of her musical background: "I liked church because life and death had such a draw for me ... What it means to live and what it means to die" (Tomita 2014). This pattern is reflected in her music, in the many times that hymn-like choral music connects to characters' nostalgia in *Cowboy Bebop* (for example, in "Green Bird" in Session 5, "Ballad of Fallen Angels").

She also entered and won composition contests from as early as second grade. In the Tomita interview, Kanno claims she "rebelled" by studying literature at Waseda University, because people expected her to study music. Kanno spent much of her young adulthood transcribing music for friends. After a childhood sheltered from jazz and popular music, she says it was her first real exposure to learning rhythm and non-classical music styles: "I'd transcribe whole sections of Al Di Meola guitar solos … You begin to learn musical mannerisms doing things like that" (Tomita 2014). Kanno joined a band and gained a reputation for "writing songs quickly," which led her to her career as a professional composer (Tomita 2014). Kanno's exploration of different genres in these years also included a trip to the United States, which she credits with giving her exposure to jazz and funk reflected in *Cowboy Bebop*.

Kanno's first compositional jobs were writing commercial jingles and scores for video games. She wrote the music for the game *Nobunaga's Ambition* and the *Uncharted Waters* series in the 1980s and early 1990s. Kanno describes how her unusual take on situations often led to unexpected musical results; for example, she wrote sad music for the princesses in *Nobunaga's Ambition*, because she was upset by their strategic marriages to older men. Even early in her career, Kanno was already cultivating a reputation for using music in unusual ways. She also describes a tendency to work from a "mental picture" when writing her scores, something she continues to do "even with anime" (Tomita 2014).

Kanno Pre-*Bebop: Macross Plus* (1994)

Kanno's break into composing for anime came with the 1994 original video animation (OVA) *Macross Plus*.[2] The four-episode series is significant for *Cowboy Bebop* in that it united the three major members of its creative team: Shinichirō Watanabe co-directed, Keiko Nobumoto wrote the screenplay, and Kanno wrote the music. As the series was a sequel to an existing popular anime, their distinct voices are not as apparent as in their later works. Still, looking at its music provides an interesting window into the tendencies that resurface throughout Yōko Kanno's career.

Music plays an important role in many *Macross* series, especially its focus on idol singers. Idols in Japan are heavily marketed and managed; young female pop stars are admired as much (if not more) for their cuteness as for their musical ability.[3] Like popular singers in the United States, idols often work in other aspects of the entertainment industry, such as acting or modeling. They have stronger expectations to maintain their image—often based on girl-next-door approachability, innocence, and availability—than their American counterparts, and, as such, their personal lives are often highly circumscribed. The concept has led to some intriguing explorations in anime, and in *Macross Plus* the idol of the moment is Sharon Apple, a hologram with artificial intelligence. Her manager, Myung Fang Lone, later reveals that Sharon's emotions and musical performances are actually her own; Myung was a famous singer before she shifted to management. This makes Sharon an even more literal manifestation of how management controls and handles idol singers. In the finale, a rogue scientist implants a microchip in Sharon that gives the idol her own consciousness. She is still based on Myung's emotional data, but can control herself, and uses her abilities to hypnotize her audiences. In the final episode of the OVA, Myung and the two men who love her, Isamu and Guld, attempt to take back control of Sharon.

Kanno was attracted to Sharon's character, including her more villainous aspects such as her ability to hypnotize and brainwash other characters. She tried to make her an "effective brainwasher" by imagining "what kinds of music might be trending in the world in the time [the year 2048] she inhabited it" (Tomita 2014). She continues, "Music tends to trend in cycles, so I thought the music in *Macross Plus* would be two cycles ahead of the current trend" (Tomita 2014), suggesting that popular music in the future will engage with music that has been popular in the past. Although she is vague on this point in the interview, the *Macross Plus* score helps to clarify this notion.

The scene in *Macross Plus* that best exemplifies Kanno's style is in episode 2, "Brain Waves," when the viewers see a full-fledged Sharon Apple concert, complete with the psychedelic, hypnotic visuals. Various styles emerge in the music here, but generally the cue can be divided into three distinct parts. The opening section is the most visually experimental, with the appearance of Sharon Apple constantly changing. The segment features intense, stunning arrays of color and disorienting use of lighting. For example, one sequence includes very rapid flashing images (which is no longer allowed in anime, after an infamous 1997 *Pokémon* episode gave some Japanese children seizures).[4] The music, called "SANTI-U," includes hip-hop effects, particularly a low, throbbing bass beat that drops at the start of the song. At 3:39 in the episode, the music shifts to electronic drone with a wordless, nasal female vocalist providing the melody. This accompanies an underwater scene, as tentacled sea creatures float across the screen, and a blue mermaid (Sharon) emerges from yellow bubbles. Around 4:27, the music speeds up, moving to a throbbing bass beat with high-pitched mallet percussion instruments, as the visuals rapidly flash between different-colored versions of Sharon. The visuals are synchronized to the rapid musical beat. At 5:33, the music dies down after building for over a minute, across increasingly colorful, unusual images, like kaleidoscope patterns and rainbow bubbles. Sharon's command center decides to switch to a new song to keep up the audience's excitement level.

This middle section of this scene uses a cue titled "Idol Talk," which is typical of 1980s dance music and features prominent synthesizer and drum beats. It is the most pop-like section of Sharon Apple's song. It features a shorthaired Sharon doing mundane tasks, like talking on the telephone. After one audience member unsuccessfully tries to hack Sharon, the music changes again, moving into the final section. This music, called "The Borderline," is breathy cabaret jazz; this is the number most similar to Kanno's work for *Cowboy Bebop*. This version of Sharon has long red hair, and she interacts directly with the audience, caressing their faces. She ends the concert doing this to main character Isamu much longer than the other characters, which foreshadows Myung's love for him. Sharon's physical performance matches the sexual nature of the music.

Like her other scores, Kanno settles on a particular musical palette for Sharon Apple: 1980s–90s techno. Both of the first two themes prominently feature electronic effects and beats. Still, she integrates other forms of music, like jazz and hip-hop, to create a style that sounds unique. Other parts of the soundtrack feature music akin to Kanno's later scores, including *Cowboy Bebop*. For example, episode 2 uses fast-paced jazz, a precursor to similar music in *Bebop*'s action sequences. Many of the personal scenes between Myung, Isamu, and Guld feature contemplative piano music that resembles the *Bebop* cues "Flying Teapot" and "Adieu" (see Chapters 6 and 7). *Macross Plus*, like *Cowboy Bebop*, features a futuristic world that is still clearly rooted in the struggles of the late twentieth century. Kanno's statement about music going "in cycles" seems to reflect this persistence of the past; the music of the future is just a different blend of pre-existing styles. Her scores establish a musical environment rooted in past traditions and contemporary practices, but differentiated via new combinations.

Clearly Kawamori also felt that the music fit the series, as Kanno continued to compose for his anime. Kanno worked with Kawamori on *Earth Girl Arjuna* (2001), the *Aquarion* series (*Genesis of Aquarion* [2005] and *Aquarion Evol* [2012]), *The Vision of Escaflowne* series (1996), and its related film, *Escaflowne* (2000); the latter two are regarded as among Kanno's most celebrated scores. This success all began with *Macross Plus*, making it of utmost importance in studying her early career.

Macross Plus sets the musical landscape heard throughout Kanno's body of work. Both Kanno and Watanabe use music in anime to create new worlds that are distinctly attuned to the needs of the stories; the music seems natural in the world of those stories. The ways that *Cowboy Bebop* achieves this naturalness are discussed in Chapters 3 and 4. For now, the discussion will turn to Kanno's post-*Bebop* stylistic evolutions through one of her major non-Watanabe soundtracks, *Wolf's Rain*.

Kanno Post-*Bebop: Wolf's Rain* (2003)

Yōko Kanno went on to work on numerous popular anime soundtracks in the years after *Cowboy Bebop*, including *Turn A Gundam* (2000) and the *Ghost in the Shell* spin-off series, *Stand Alone Complex* (2002–3). All of these scores reflect different elements of her background and style, especially her deftness at combining disparate genres into new ones. The most fascinating Kanno work to consider in the shadow of *Cowboy Bebop*, none the less, is *Wolf's Rain*. The two series share many narrative similarities, in spite of sharp differences in setting and tone. Keiko Nobumoto served as head of the story team for both *Bebop* and *Wolf's Rain*, and both works share many of Nobumoto's pet themes and narrative quirks.

Nobumoto has a knack for writing characters who are doomed by the constraints of their societies, in spite (or because) of their striving against those constraints. Her writing can be very cynical, even with contrasting emotional tones. *Wolf's Rain* tends to be more sentimental than *Bebop*, and many major characters suffer harsher endings. Still, the story is very powerful and engaging from the beginning of the series, thanks to the complex apocalyptic world and vivid, endearing characters.

The series follows a group of wolves and humans in a bleak, dystopian future. The wolves are believed to have become extinct from over-hunting but have managed to survive by disguising themselves as human beings and living on the margins of human civilization. They come to the city when human scientists create Cheza, a flower maiden who is connected to the wolves' search for a paradise in the face of their crumbling world. The human scientists pursue the wolves when they break Cheza out of the laboratory and take her with them on their journey. Other humans, called nobles, chase after paradise for their own nefarious reasons. The anime results in a confrontation between one of the nobles and the wolves with the flower maiden, whom he needs to open paradise and remake the humans' crumbling world in the nobles' own image.

Wolf's Rain is a complicated, metaphorical tale with references to a variety of Western and Eastern philosophies and mythologies. The world is reclaimed by nature as human civilization falls into decline, and much of the series is spent trekking through lush northern forests with the wolves. Kanno's music reflects this dichotomy between two different worlds: the wild animal world versus the decadence of human civilization.

Kanno's score for *Wolf's Rain* includes lush orchestral music, often used for tragic or bittersweet scenes. What makes it distinct is its heavy use of what is understood to be traditional music from cultures around the world. Kanno's score includes traditional Japanese instruments like *shakuhachi* (end-blown bamboo flute), North Indian sitars, Spanish flamenco guitar music, Celtic and Appalachian fiddle tunes, and medieval European music. The last may reflect Kanno's affinity to Christian music, which she described in the Tomita interview as a primitive emotion. She noted, "I feel religious music, to Europeans, is one of the first forms of music they come in contact with—music that becomes the foundations for their beliefs and life" (Tomita 2014).

These "traditional" musical genres have those associations in film music that make them work in the context of *Wolf's Rain*. In particular, their relatively simple textures (requiring only a few instruments at a time) allow them to stand in contrast to the full symphonic instrumentation in other parts of the score.

Mood differences also mark these two instrumentations of Kanno's *Wolf's Rain* score. The orchestral music expresses strong, dramatic emotions, usually tragic, as is appropriate for its use in emotionally devastating scenes. The traditional music in the soundtrack is gentler and more irreverent, giving off a mysterious or playful air and accompanying moments when the characters are exploring or relaxing instead of getting into confrontations. When the traditional music is used in scenes that are more dramatic, the mood is more ambiguous, and the scenes relate to the uneasy relationship between humans and the natural world (represented by the wolves). One poignant moment in episode 2, which introduces Toboe, the youngest and most naïve wolf, comes with the use of a medieval-sounding track full of modal harmonies and low flutes. Succumbing to his wolf instincts, Toboe kills the pet hawk of a human friend, and he quickly realizes that's not what his human friend wanted. The friend stares in shock at his explanation as she notices Toboe's human appearance is an illusion.

The series soundtrack contains far more than these genres. It is as eclectic as any other Kanno soundtrack, featuring touches of jazz and stirring rock ballads. One such cue, "Heaven's Not Enough" (sung by Steve Conte), plays a key role in the final episodes of the series. It incorporates the low flutes used throughout the series into its power ballad. This ballad is reminiscent of Led Zeppelin's "Stairway to Heaven"—fitting, given the search for Paradise that dominates the series.

The relationship between traditional music and Western symphonic music—representing the height of musical "civilization"—reinforces that civilization is dying in the world of *Wolf's Rain*, and that nature is reasserting itself. The true answers for its characters come from returning to that nature.

Liveness and Authenticity

Kanno uses music to explore the interaction between live performance and recorded music. As discussed in Chapter 3, *Cowboy Bebop* uses musical genre to explore "authenticity" among its characters. Musicians who played for Kanno told me that the focus on "authenticity" bled into the recording studio. Both Steve Conte and Emily Bindiger, who sings on "Flying Teapot" and "Adieu," told me that Kanno recorded their songs live, with all the instruments. Other composers they worked with recorded each instrument separately, using as many takes as possible. Instead, Kanno put all the instruments and singers for a track in one room, and recorded them all live, in one or as few takes as possible.

Steve Conte recounted that, when he recorded "Call Me Call Me," "[Kanno] played piano herself live, and she had these thirty strings—violins, violas, cellos, basses—everybody playing live with her, and me singing live … I guess she wanted the feeling, and I'm glad she did it this way, because it was like the experience of a lifetime. I never recorded live with strings. Only people like Frank Sinatra do that!" (Conte, interview). Similarly, Emily Bindiger said:

> There was a pianist, flugelhorn, and myself—separated, but we could see each other, in live take after live take. Which is why some of my notes are a little off, pitchy, but she liked the take … . I would have preferred to do it over, but … she thought it was real, she thought it told a story, and I agree with her. If things tell a story and have the right performance, you can forgive some off notes. And it made for a very in-the-moment performance. "I better try to get this right, but tell the story, and relay the intent of her songs." (Emily Bindiger, Skype interview with the author, May 31, 2016)

Neither of them clarified whether she followed this pattern as consistently for other soundtracks, though Conte also worked on music for *Wolf's Rain*. Still, these anecdotes speak to the raw emotional power that is associated with Kanno's music.

As Bindiger noted, Kanno's insistence on liveness in recording the *Cowboy Bebop* soundtrack shows a preference for rawness and authenticity over technical perfection. This authenticity could explain why her music succeeds at touching people and telling the stories of complicated, imperfect characters as they struggle through life.

Conclusion

While Yōko Kanno prefers certain genres over others, it is still hard to pin down what defines her style. Unlike other composers with distinct musical voices, Kanno is mostly notable for her refusal to define herself by the usual vocabulary associated with style. Most of her fans, including many of the musicians she has worked with, love her music for its eclecticism.

In looking at her broader career, one can none the less isolate distinct traits. It is not just her stylistic diversity, but the way she uses that diversity. Kanno is well aware of the associations that different musical genres have for her audiences, and she plays with them in a way that interacts with an anime's themes and narrative.

This genre awareness is what has made her an ideal collaborator of Shinichirō Watanabe. He is not the only director with whom she has frequently worked; her resume is also filled with works with other directors, most notably Shōji Kawamori. Still, the frequent collaborations with Watanabe suggest that the two share certain sensibilities, such as an awareness of the importance of the role of music in film in telling a story. Both are also attuned to the nuances of musical genre. The following chapter examines the ways in which *Cowboy Bebop* plays with musical genre.

3 "Black Dog" Serenade: *Bebop*, Classic Rock, and Jazz Standards

Referenced Sessions
#6 Sympathy for the Devil
#7 Heavy Metal Queen

At a concert at the 2013 Otakon convention in Baltimore, Maryland, Kanno was introduced as the "master of all musical genres." However, in an interview for the now-defunct website Ex.org, Kanno expressed a different perspective on her reputation: "I hear everyone talk about how many genres [I work in] like classical, jazz and others, but personally, I don't divide music by genre when creating … When I create music, I don't consider at all what genere [*sic*] I like best, but what the scene or anime calls for, like a love [theme] or mood … There isn't one genre I like more than the others." While she confirms her collaborators' description of her as a musical chameleon, her assertion that she doesn't write with "genre" in mind seems to contradict the essence of *Cowboy Bebop*, a score so seemingly preoccupied with genre.

Whether Kanno intended it or not, *Cowboy Bebop* shows a strong awareness of subgenres of classic jazz and rock. This is obvious without even hearing a note of the soundtrack, simply by looking at the titles of the different sessions. Chosen by Watanabe, they reflect iconic rock songs and albums, including those by the Rolling Stones, Bob Dylan, Led Zeppelin, Queen, and KISS. They also include references to blues, jazz, dance styles (shuffle, ballad, waltz, elegy, samba), and subgenres (heavy metal, boogie-woogie, funk). Bebop forms the series title. The only session without a specifically musical title is session 20, "Pierrot le Fou," which takes its name from a film; however, Watanabe told us that it was also inspired by the song "Mad Pierrot" by the Japanese technopop group Yellow Magic Orchestra, one of his favorites as a teenager (Watanabe, interview). Therefore, every session title makes a reference, in some manner, to music. This feature initially drew me, a classic-rock obsessed teenager, to the series. Clearly, *Cowboy Bebop* nods to people with broad musical tastes.

In spite of the references to songs and albums in session titles, the score for *Cowboy Bebop* does not use the works it references, which would require copyright clearance. There are only a handful of instances of pre-existing music in its soundtrack, none of them involving the artists, songs, or albums referenced in the titles. *Cowboy Bebop*'s original soundtrack instead references the different musics embodied in its session titles in a less overt way. Given the lack of the actual music, these insistent musical references in the titles seem a curious choice, inviting one to explore the music in the series. While many anime series employ jazz or classic-rock influenced music, few repeatedly remind the audience of their musical influences in the way that *Cowboy Bebop* does.

This chapter explores the meaning behind the invocation of these jazz, blues, and classic rock standards in the series. It looks at how these genres emerge in the soundtrack, and why they are important to the artistic goals of this series. It looks at the ways musical genre shapes the characters and story, as well as its significance as a framing device for the series. Issues discussed include genre and authenticity, real-world functionality of musical genre, and expectations of the use of certain genres in film (and the ways in which *Cowboy Bebop* confirms and/or subverts these expectations). It will examine just what this music means for the crew of the *Bebop* and the many people they encounter in the late twenty-first-century solar system.

List of Specific Musical References in Cowboy Bebop Session Titles

- #2 Stray Dog Strut: The Stray Cats' "Stray Cat Strut" from their 1981 self-titled debut album
- #3 Honky Tonk Women: The Rolling Stones' 1969 hit single of the same name
- #6 Sympathy for the Devil: The Rolling Stones' song from their 1968 album, *Beggars Banquet*
- #9 Jamming with Edward: relatively obscure 1972 Rolling Stones album *Jamming with Edward!*, comprised of long, free jams recorded during the *Exile on Main Street* sessions
- #11 Toys in the Attic: Aerosmith's 1975 album
- #14 Bohemian Rhapsody: Queen's 1975 hit single, from *A Night at the Opera*
- #15 My Funny Valentine: song from 1937 Rodgers & Hart musical *Babes in Arms*, which became a jazz standard that was covered by Chet Baker, Duke Ellington, Ella Fitzgerald, Frank Sinatra, and Miles Davis, among others

- #16 Black Dog Serenade: Led Zeppelin's 1971 single "Black Dog," the opening track on *Led Zeppelin IV*
- #18 Speak like a Child: Herbie Hancock's 1968 album
- #19 Wild Horses: The Rolling Stones' 1971 single, from *Sticky Fingers*
- #20 Pierrot le Fou: The title comes from the 1965 film by Jean-Luc Godard, part of the French New Wave. Watanabe was also inspired by the song "Mad Pierrot" by Yellow Magic Orchestra, from their eponymous 1978 album.
- #24 Hard Luck Woman: KISS's 1976 single, from *Rock and Roll Over*
- #25–6 The Real Folk Blues: Chess Records' 1965–7 compilation albums of their major blues artists, including John Lee Hooker, Muddy Waters, Sonny Boy Williamson II, and Howlin' Wolf. The Muddy Waters albums are the best known.
- *Cowboy Bebop the Movie: Knockin' on Heaven's Door*: Bob Dylan's 1973 single from his soundtrack for the movie *Pat Garrett and Billy the Kid*.

The Blues (and Blues-Rock): Music of Authenticity and Experience

Music plays a large role in session six, "Sympathy for the Devil," defining both characters who appear only in this episode and major ones recurring throughout the series. The session centers on Wenn, a vicious old man stuck in a prepubescent body. He manages to lure a series of male caretakers to commit crimes with him, knowing they'll be accused instead of the innocent child—and this pattern holds, despite his current victims' warnings before he kills them. Spike finally figures it out toward the end of the session and kills Wenn. Though it's not obvious at first glance, music plays an important role in establishing the different characters' relationships to age and experience.

The first clue that this little boy is more than who he seems comes when Jet and Spike first see him play the harmonica (or the "blues harp," as Jet calls it) on-stage in a dive bar. Jet is shocked that this little boy plays the instrument "like an old blues man," showing not just technical proficiency but also much more soul than he would expect from someone of Wenn's apparent age (session 6, 02:48). His comment jives with what audiences often expect of child prodigies—technically masterful but low on the emotion that comes from life experiences. As the blues often speak to hard times and adult experiences like poverty, drinking, and conjugal love, it is difficult to imagine a naïve child as a blues master. That Wenn is not only drawn to the genre but has also made a name for himself in it suggests that he's not as young as he looks. In case the audience doesn't pick up on these musical discourses, Jet makes them explicit.

This scene also establishes Jet's own love of the blues. Jet and Spike discuss Wenn's performance in the following scene. Spike is surprised by how much Jet "love[s] that blues harp," and counters, "I thought you liked jazz." "Don't be dense," Jet responds. "I started wailing the blues when they smacked my bottom the day I was born." Spike is amused by this statement, and responds in a way that notes the inherent absurdity of it: "A baby hipster. Very cool!" Once again, this conversation reinforces the idea that blues is the music of age and experience, and so the idea that a young child would be "wailing the blues" doesn't make a lot of sense. Jet's love of the blues also ties into his characterization as older and more experienced, having lived a rough life from which he has learned a great deal. We see glimpses into his troubled past in his focus episodes (session 10, "Ganymede Elegy," and session 16, "Black Dog Serenade," covered in more detail in Chapter 6) but even before them, Jet is defined in the group as a wise, sage-like, fatherly figure to his younger shipmates. It is telling that he would like the blues.

Wenn also turns out to be someone who has seen a great deal in his long lifetime. He lived on Earth in the 2010s at the time of a "gate explosion," an undefined disaster which made much of Earth uninhabitable. He saw his family destroyed before his eyes, and the effect of the explosion on his body, along with later scientific experiments, made him forever young. Since then, he has moved around the solar system, leaving before others become suspicious of his eternal youth. (Still, his blues career means Jet and Spike were able to uncover articles about him from decades ago in which he appears unchanged.) Wenn's love of the blues further establishes it as the music of authentic life experience—a tough, long life, with a wide variety of experiences.

Notably, Spike rejects this music later in the episode, after killing Wenn. Spike takes Wenn's harmonica, throws it up in the air and pretends to shoot it, pointing his finger and saying, "Bang." (This visually foreshadows Spike's final scene in the series, in session 26, "The Real Folk Blues (Part 2)," where he presumably meets his death at the hands of his nemesis Vicious.) Spike literally tosses away Wenn's harmonica (22:43)—the cultural marker of the blues, the authenticity that defines Wenn and is appreciated by Jet—even though Spike himself has lived a hard life as a repentant gangster. Perhaps

Spike's rejection of the blues and preference for faster, more danceable music (like the big band jazz that characterizes his fight scenes) shows his determination *not* to grow old. We see this behavior in Spike's refusal to learn from his mistakes, in his easy-come, easy-go attitude, and the fact that these traits presumably lead him to an early grave at the end of the series. That fundamental change is not a viable option for Spike or the other characters reinforces the apparent authenticity of the blues and its association with a long, hard-lived life.

The episode's discourses about the blues—what the genre says, what sort of person enjoys it—make it all the more interesting to examine the episode's title, "Sympathy for the Devil." The Rolling Stones' song title partly reflects the plot; the major characters initially feel sympathy for Wenn before they realize that he's a devil in disguise. The title also resonates with the episode's musical themes, given the song's place in the Rolling Stones' discography. "Sympathy for the Devil" is the first track on the 1968 album, *Beggars Banquet*, which was the beginning of the Stones' major shift away from the psychedelic rock that prevailed at the time toward the late-1960s style that came to be known as roots rock.

Roots rock shifted away from the experimental, genre-defying features of psychedelic rock back toward the roots of rock in country and blues. The Rolling Stones became leaders of this movement, and their time in it featured a string of critically acclaimed albums including *Beggars Banquet*, *Let It Bleed* (1969), *Sticky Fingers* (1971), and *Exile on Main Street* (1972). All of the Stones references in *Cowboy Bebop*'s session titles come from this period and style. "Honky Tonk Women" is a single from the *Let It Bleed* era and heavily features country music instrumentation, like cowbell and steel guitar; "Wild Horses" is another country-style track from *Sticky Fingers*; and

"Jamming with Edward" is the name of an album of outtakes from the *Exile on Main Street* sessions. The focus on this era of the Stones' music, when they looked to recreate and remake the music of Delta blues masters like Robert Johnson, parallels the show's discourse on the blues. To deepen the association, one of the Jet-centered episodes, "Black Dog Serenade," takes its name from "Black Dog" (1971) by Led Zeppelin, another group heavily influenced by the blues.

Why would *Cowboy Bebop* name its episodes after rock's interpretations of blues music instead of the real thing? These names seem to contrast with the blues' association with authenticity; the Rolling Stones' and Led Zeppelin's versions of the blues are rarely seen as authentic and are often discussed as examples of cultural appropriation in rock.[1]

Cultural appropriation is a cultural value in and of itself. Not every culture views concepts such as race, authenticity, and ownership the same way. Much of Japan's popular music in the last century involves the adoption and adaptation of global influences, and its pop culture similarly influences that of other countries.[2] For example, anime is influenced by American animation and cinema, and its popularity in the West has led to its influence in Western popular media. Like popular music, anime is a transnational phenomenon.

Another explanation is that the Rolling Stones and other classic rock artists are simply better known to audiences (both Japanese and American) than most Delta and Chicago blues artists. Referencing these names endows the series with the trappings of rock 'n' roll coolness—rebellion, drugs, sex. Fans of the Stones would likely appreciate *Cowboy Bebop*'s rock- and blues-filled soundtrack, which shows Yōko Kanno's own appreciation for American and British classic rock.

The soundtrack itself pays direct homage to the styles of the blues artists who influenced groups like the Stones and Zeppelin. Many of the blues tracks in the soundtrack feature acoustic guitar and harmonica, often including long variations on the same basic melody or harmonic pattern. This is true of "Spokey Dokey" (the music that Wenn plays and which appears in other places throughout the series), "Digging My Potato," and "Forever Broke," the primary acoustic-blues pieces in the series. There are also more rock-oriented tracks, particularly those sung by Steve Conte (such as "Call Me Call Me" and "Rain"), but the blues predominates in these episodes named for their rock descendants.[3] Many of the tracks labeled blues (such as "Cat Blues," "Farewell Blues," and "The Real Folk Blues") feature instrumentation closer to jazz or R&B.

Problematizing these ideas of authenticity in blues and jazz fits with *Cowboy Bebop*'s overall project. To paraphrase several commercial bumpers in the series, anime is "a genre itself" through its blending and reinterpreting of standard genres. It makes its characters seem like they've lived hard-fought lives while challenging cultural norms about what is real or authentic—not only with Wenn's appearance or Spike's behavior, but even with Jet, who is not nearly as old as viewers would expect from his character and the life he's lived. As he reveals in the next-episode preview for "Waltz for Venus," he is only 36! *Cowboy Bebop* is all about challenging the way we think about genre and the baggage that comes with those boundaries, including discourses of authenticity.[4] In "Sympathy for the Devil," appearances do not always match reality, and the series plays on our expectations regarding the music we associate with those appearances. Wenn does not look like a blues master, because he is not who he appears to be. Jet loves the blues, but he is younger than we think, too.

On a broader level, *Cowboy Bebop* arguably stretches expectations with its manipulation of film genre, too, expanding viewers' ideas of what a science fiction story can do.

Among the session and soundtrack titles, one makes an important homage to classic blues artists—"The Real Folk Blues." The session and track (which serves as the ending theme throughout the series) take their name from a series of compilation albums featuring major Chicago blues artists, most famously Muddy Waters. Even there, they problematize the norms of what counts as authentic blues. "The Real Folk Blues" is a jazzed-up ballad, not a blues song, with the "blues" aesthetic reflected instead in its melancholy lyrics.

From Angelic Ballads to Big-Band Battles: Cowboy Bebop and Jazz

As evident from the series title, the other genre from which *Cowboy Bebop* draws its inspiration is jazz. Examples include the jazz standard "My Funny Valentine," Herbie Hancock's album *Speak like a Child*, and genre or dance names like the shuffle and boogie-woogie. Jazz is the dominant genre on the *Bebop* soundtrack, and helps to establish the series' themes and aesthetics. Kanno was clear in her email that Watanabe instructed her to write "four-beat jazz," which she did, despite not thinking the anime "would sell with jazz." She added she recently learned he did not mean the specific music "so much as the spirit of jazz and the lifestyle of jazz musicians," but still prepared many "jazz-like songs to address his request" (Kanno, email communication).

In contrast to the blues, which tends to represent age and experience, jazz is the music of exuberance in the series. Jazz is featured in Spike's and, to a lesser extent, Faye's music. (As discussed in Chapter 6, Faye's musical signature is ambiguous for reasons that are important to her character.) It is also the music of sophistication, often used diegetically when the characters enter classy establishments such as upscale bars, casinos, or urban high-rises. Jazz is ubiquitous in Japanese culture (Atkins 2001), and, as in the United States, is often played in commercial establishments to lend an air of sophistication and coolness.

One of the more curious uses of jazz in *Cowboy Bebop*, and one that recurs over and over, is its use in climactic battle scenes. These selections tend to feature big bands, such as in "Rush," "New York Rush," and "Too Good Too Bad." There is an aural contrast between the quieter, more sparsely orchestrated ballads and the cabaret-style songs that make up some of the other recurring jazz cues. It might be puzzling that music usually associated with cosmopolitan sophistication would be chosen for a battle scene. In anime and American television, battle music tends to follow certain patterns, often with epic orchestral or hard-rock instrumentation, rather than big-band jazz, even though the ensembles are similarly large and sonorous.

For *Cowboy Bebop*, the jazz setting actually makes perfect sense, given the ways in which these battles play out. The style of the action sequences is very dancelike, from Spike's fluid, martial arts style of physical fighting (which is so riveting that another character begs Spike for a tutorial in "Waltz for Venus," session 8), to the balletic movement of the ships in the space battles. The big-band jazz accompaniment reflects the graceful, musical quality of these movements, whether the bodies in motion be Spike or the ships. *Cowboy Bebop*'s action sequences bring to mind the similarities that numerous film scholars have discovered between the action sequence and song numbers in film musicals; they are visual spectacles that take viewers outside of the narrative (even when they advance it) and focus on a sort of bodily virtuosity through either fighting or dancing.[5] *Cowboy Bebop*'s direction and use of music in its action sequences further reflects this ambiguity.

The title of the series itself, *Cowboy Bebop*, also clearly references a specific moment in jazz history. Bebop in the 1940s with Charlie Parker, Dizzy Gillespie, and Thelonious Monk bridged two perceptions of jazz—as popular dance music and as art music. While preserving the danceable qualities of earlier jazz such as swing, bebop moved jazz in increasingly experimental directions, putting it in a transitional position in the history of jazz. As E. Taylor Atkins details in *Blue Nippon*, his seminal book on Japanese jazz, bebop plays a particularly important role in Japan's engagement with the musical genre; it was the prevailing style when Japan re-emerged on the worldwide jazz scene during the Occupation, and Japan's jazz musicians felt the need to play catch-up with these new trends (Atkins 2001: 165–220). Atkins writes, "Having won the freedom to play their beloved jazz openly in less circumscribed contexts than ever before, Japanese were truly bewildered to discover that the music had passed them by. And with the bebop ethos of 'continual innovation,' the music was guaranteed to change again, necessitating constant vigilance and study to stay current" (2001: 197). Nevertheless, Atkins continues to note that bebop's status as "an 'art music' for a more intellectual audience" did change the contexts of jazz performance in Japanese youth culture, where it had been primarily oriented around dance halls. Bebop "displac[ed] dance halls and [gave] birth to swanky cabarets, coffee-houses, and after-hours dives for which there had been few if any pre-war precedents" (2001: 197). What other music could better define *Cowboy Bebop*, the work that aims to "become a new genre itself"? In a decade of groundbreaking, thematically rich anime that demonstrated the genre's potential as high art (such as Hideaki Anno's *Neon Genesis Evangelion* [1995–6] and Kunihiko Ikuhara's *Revolutionary Girl Utena* [1997]), *Cowboy Bebop* makes itself the transitional anime between those more serious works and lighter sci-fi action spectacle. It is art on the cusp of something new, just like bebop.

In his interview with the series editor, Watanabe detailed his thoughts about the bebop genre, and how those fit into his goals for *Cowboy Bebop*:

> In the history of jazz, bebop was a turning point from swing and other older styles. Those old styles had a score, and the musicians would play according to the score. But after Charlie Parker, in bebop, players threw away the score and played freely. They wanted to express themselves freely and started to improvise a lot. I respect and like that kind of music. *Cowboy Bebop*'s characters are like those musicians: they are free, and I want them to act in an improvisatory way. The staff (for *Cowboy Bebop*) were also like bebop musicians. We didn't want to make anime in a pattern that was already set. So I gave it that title. (Watanabe, interview)

For Watanabe, bebop signified freedom. His attachment to the genre explains why it would be associated with scenes where the characters really let themselves go and act "free," as is often the case in the battle scenes.

As for Kanno, jazz meant "talk[ing] about your troubles for which there's no solution." She also believed jazz to be versatile; relaying a memory of watching a jazz funeral in

New Orleans, she found the music "expressed every aspect of life, including resignation, grief, and intimacy" (Kanno, email communication).

A Musical Shock to the System: "Heavy Metal Queen"

To examine *Cowboy Bebop*'s engagement with musical genre, it is helpful to discuss events during which the series deviates from its musical tendencies toward blues and jazz (see Chapter 5, "Cowboy Funk" and "Mushroom Samba"). Another important example of this deviation is session 7, "Heavy Metal Queen."

Heavy metal plays a strong role in this episode, with the signature track of the session, "Live in Baghdad," clearly standing out. It begins with a loud, fast guitar riff, announcing the shift in genre from the get-go. Characteristic of metal, the vocal style is screaming and shouting, and other harsh timbres abound. Despite the provocative title, the lyrics have nothing to do with Baghdad and are mostly nonsensical. As *Cowboy Bebop* came out after the Gulf War and before 9/11, it is difficult to know what the intentions were in the song title other than reflecting a loud, raucous place. It is similar to the surface invocation of real-life places, seen in the lyrics of "Mushroom Hunting."

"Heavy Metal Queen" focuses on the character of V.T., a brusque female trucker who encourages others to bet on guessing her full name. (Only Spike gets it right, at the end of the episode.) She also despises bounty hunters, due to her personal baggage; her late husband was a famous one. None the less, she's a generally good-natured person, always on the lookout for underdogs while accompanied by her cat. As Simon Abrams writes in his review of the episode for the *A.V. Club*, "V.T. considers chivalry to be a non-negotiable virtue. When bounty hunters try to rape a waitress at the bar Spike is recovering from a hangover in, V.T. comes to her rescue" (2011). This sense of duty to the less fortunate gets V.T. entangled in Spike and Faye's latest attempt to collect a bounty. She can set aside her bias against their profession to help those in need.

V.T. is a female version of the "rough, rural, working-class man with a heart of gold" archetype. Despite *Cowboy Bebop*'s many impoverished characters—including the *Bebop* crew themselves, for much of the series—this type of person is rare, as they usually have some degree of the exotic or sophisticated about them, like hipsters who fell on hard times. V.T. is decidedly unglamorous, and lives out a "rough" life decidedly different from that of Jet or Wenn. The darkest part of V.T.'s past is about whom she married, not necessarily anything she did herself. Other than her grudge against bounty hunters, it does not seem to affect her; V.T. keeps an optimism and heroism that is completely alien to characters like Jet and Spike, in spite of her gruff exterior.

Her love of heavy metal also appears to be a part of that misleading outward image. "Live in Baghdad" moves between being diegetic and non-diegetic in its various appearances during "Heavy Metal Queen." It starts as the former, used to illustrate the colorful exterior of V.T.'s truck-spaceship. Later in the episode, V.T. plays it from her truck stereo as Spike and Faye hitch a ride to track down their target, Decker. As expected, the jazzy main characters are not so fond of V.T.'s choice of music, especially since they have to scream over it in order to talk to each other. Faye, fed up, finally yells at V.T. to "please turn down that repulsive music!" V.T. schools her by defining it as "heavy metal, by the way," and adds, "It's *not* repulsive—it's very soothing!" It is expected that V.T. would defend her musical taste after Faye insults it, but the reason she gives is unexpected. For most listeners, even metal fans, "soothing" would be the last word to come to mind about metal, and viewers might assume that V.T.'s love for it reflects her rough, tough image. Instead, her reason for liking it suggests she needs comforting; she's not so rough a person after all.

The episode "Heavy Metal Queen," like "Sympathy for the Devil" preceding it, plays with viewers' expectations, teaching that appearances can be deceiving. Faye assumes that a grizzly tattooed guy she's been tracking is Decker, her target, but only realizes at the last minute that Decker is the bespectacled nerd she asked for assistance earlier. V.T. also upends viewers' expectations of gender roles, both in her large size, lack of stereotypical feminine markers (with her short hair, deeper voice and casual, cowboy-style clothing), and her profession as a trucker. In Abrams's review, both he and many of his reader-commenters initially assumed that V.T. was a man, even though V.T.'s voice actors in both Japanese and English are women—Tomie Kataoka and Melodee Spevacek. The session also upends our expectations about heavy metal. It is not always for head-banging or moshing. Some people find it soothing.

As its treatment of blues, jazz, and heavy metal makes clear, *Cowboy Bebop* is a series that is intimately aware of the expectations of genre. Its subtitle, "the work that becomes a new genre itself," suggests that it attempts to problematize them. The trailblazing soundtrack challenges the associations viewers have with musical genres, particularly the blues and jazz.

4 "Jupiter Jazz": Scoring the World of *Bebop*

Referenced Sessions
#1 Asteroid Blues
#2 Stray Dog Strut
#8 Waltz for Venus
#20 Pierrot le Fou

Referenced External Works
Trigun (1998)

Up to "Waltz for Venus" (session 8), the world of *Cowboy Bebop* has been shown as glamorous, urban, and harsh. It's a world of sleazy bars, casinos, and tough people who might kill you if you get in the way of their crime syndicate, and even the heroes need to adapt to these edges. "Waltz for Venus" serves as a turning point for rounding out the setting of *Cowboy Bebop*. The Venus the characters visit still has troubles—some major ones—but it is peaceful compared to the world that the characters have traversed so far.

From the beginning, the visual and musical aesthetics establish the serenity of Venus compared to other worlds. The cinematography plays a key role, particularly the use of colors. Venus's atmosphere is full of bright yellows and oranges during the daytime, and reds and pinks at night, contrasting it with the bluer colors of other, less harmonious planets and moons.[1] Even in the more violent or disturbing scenes, e.g., when Faye threatens men in a bar, there's a soft, hazy effect to the *mise en scène*.[2] The musical choices in "Waltz for Venus" also play an important role in this characterization. In contrast with the loud, bombastic jazz and rock that has defined *Cowboy Bebop* up to this point—and especially in the preceding session, "Heavy Metal Queen"—"Waltz for Venus" uses solo harmonica wails and other slow-tempo music with pared-down instrumentation. One of its key scenes features a tinny music box playing "Stella By Moor"; it sounds like a lullaby. Later in the series, this somber ballad becomes "The Singing Sea" in Jet's focus episodes. Even the jazz number in the climactic battle scene is noticeably subdued compared to the usual scoring for these moments. It features only a solo saxophone and a rhythm section, as opposed to the brass-heavy big bands Kanno typically uses in these sequences, such as "Too Good Too Bad" from session 4 ("Gateway Shuffle"). The marked difference between Venus and other planets in the solar system is realized visually and sonically in this episode. This variety of different societies, cultures, and atmospheres is a feature of *Cowboy Bebop*'s primary genre: the space western.

The term "space western" describes shows that feature traveling spaceships and exploring new worlds, based on and using aesthetics from traditional narratives about the American West. Anime sci-fi includes more than a few notable space westerns, both before (*Outlaw Star*, 1998) and after (*Space Dandy*) *Cowboy Bebop*. Some, like *Trigun* (1998), took a more literal approach to the "western," setting its series on a Wild West-like planet, rather than having its characters travel from place to place. Others take their "movement" from the going-from-place-to-place model more than (or along with) the western aesthetic. *Cowboy Bebop* firmly fits within the latter group.

While *Star Trek* (1966–) is often framed as the prototypical space western in Western media, its influence on anime is limited; even in the United States it did not become popular until later syndication of the Original Series (1966–8), and *Star Trek* never quite took off in Japan the way that it did in the U.S. More likely influential upon series like *Cowboy Bebop* is the *Star Wars* franchise (1977–), which shares the traveling-to-different-worlds element even if it tends to be classed as "space opera." Watanabe made it clear that he saw *Star Wars* as a sci-fi model, explaining how he intended to differentiate *Cowboy Bebop* from it: "*Cowboy Bebop* doesn't involve grand heroes like *Star Wars*, but people in modest spaceships, on back roads. It's in outer space, but I wanted it to be jazz, a kind of space jazz. But at the same time, I wanted to avoid having music that sounded stereotypically like 'space music'" (Watanabe, interview). *Cowboy Bebop* may be different from a typical sci-fi story, in music and narrative content; still, like more traditional space westerns/opera, it needs to distinguish between its many different, colorful worlds.

Most sci-fi series create clear visual distinctions between different planets but vary in their approaches to each world's sonic palette. On the one hand, show-runners may prefer to keep the musical styles consistent rather than varying them across planets, because of the key role of music in setting affective states. (For example, the American TV series *Firefly* [2002] takes this approach, whereby Joss Whedon uses a primarily bluegrass soundtrack no matter where its characters go.) On the other hand, music can be an important way to illustrate the differences between environments, especially planets that are markedly different from the ones that the main characters (and, by extension, the viewers) normally visit. A sudden burst of unusual or unfamiliar music can easily illustrate a fish-out-of-water feeling.

Cowboy Bebop falls in the middle of this spectrum in its approaches to music and setting. As discussed in earlier chapters, the series uses music partly to establish its place within broader genres, including westerns and gangster films, requiring some musical consistency across sessions. It also uses music to refer back to earlier sessions, and other similarities between disparate parts of its story, especially to illustrate the trajectories that characters take in the series (explained further in Chapters 6 and 7). Still another key part of *Cowboy Bebop* is establishing the world(s) of the late twenty-first century that are urban, sophisticated, edgy, but above all, diverse. Music is important to establishing this diversity of settings, across people and cultures, and especially across worlds.

The series lacks non-human aliens, which distinguishes it from exploration-oriented science fiction. *Cowboy Bebop* presents a world of planets terraformed by and for human beings, with cultures derived from Earth's ethnic and national groups. It has less of the musical exoticism used in other series to suggest alien creatures. *Cowboy Bebop*'s diversity of planets mirrors the diversity of human cultures and ecological environments, which, in turn, beget different soundscapes peculiar to these settings.

The music of *Cowboy Bebop* shows an awareness of music's cultural associations in present-day Japan and the industrialized West. In order to make associations between the rough streets of Ganymede and those of present-day cities, *Cowboy Bebop* has to set that scene in a way that viewers will recognize, with familiar musical tropes. While visuals and plot details play a key role in setting that scene, music also establishes a particular place. The first session, "Asteroid Blues," illustrates this effect in its depiction of the Tijuana asteroid colony.

Case Study #1: "Asteroid Blues"

"Asteroid Blues" sets up many of the conventions in the series. Viewers are introduced to Spike and Jet, the two members of the *Bebop* crew at this point (Ein joins in the following session, Faye in sessions 3–4, and Edward in session 9). They are also introduced to the titular ship and the characters' mission as bounty hunters. Spike and Jet are headed to an asteroid called Tijuana, which recalls the actual city on the California–Mexico border. The Tijuana in the series is a dead-end place, full of seedy bars and people looking to move on to better lives elsewhere. Katerina—the girlfriend of their target, Asimov—frequently expresses a desire to use their drug-dealing money to start their lives over on Mars. While this portrayal may seem a negative stereotype of border-town life, the setting does help to establish the tone and major themes of the series. The main characters of *Cowboy Bebop* are all trying to escape their pasts in one way or another, and, like Katerina, they rarely succeed.

It also initiates many of the musical conventions of the series. "Asteroid Blues" uses the scoring associated with cowboy westerns, full of acoustic guitars and harmonicas, to establish this place as the backwoods of the late twenty-first century. The action sequences feature fast-paced, big-band jazz, as in the track "Rush" in this episode. Another motif is "ELM," a folk-like melody on acoustic guitar that becomes a symbol for regrets and broken dreams. It plays as Katerina reveals her plan to Spike, and he tells her that she can't just run away. Spike is shown to be right. Near the end of the episode, Katerina says to Asimov, "We'll never get out of here now. I'll never see Mars." She realizes that shackling herself to Asimov has destroyed her dreams rather than achieving them. When Asimov breaks down from all the drugs he's doing, she shoots him, then destroys their ship and herself. Considered in the context of its other uses in the series, "ELM" foreshadows Katerina's death. This cue recurs in another meditation on broken dreams, in session 10, "Ganymede Elegy" (Chapter 6). It also establishes the relevant neighborhood of Ganymede as a seedy place, full of dead ends and cruel mistakes.

On the other hand, "Rush" is only used for one memorable action sequence in the session, as Spike fights Asimov. *Cowboy Bebop* is well-known for its brassy, jazzy soundtrack, so why does it wait until the very end of that first episode to reveal the ace in its hand? It's because the sophisticated, urban jazz sounds don't fit the remote asteroid of Tijuana. The western scoring establishes the asteroid as a desolate, sad place. The jazz represents Spike and the way that his actions interrupt and overwhelm the atmosphere of Tijuana.

Cowboy Bebop uses many western cues ("Spokey Dokey," "Felt Tip Pen," "Don't Bother None") in various forms throughout the series. Rarely, though, does it stack so many in one episode. Typically, there is one harmonica/acoustic-guitar theme per session, unless it is going for an earthy, western feel with a particular world of character (such as with the harmonica-playing focus character of session 6, "Sympathy for the Devil"). The use of so many of these cues in "Asteroid Blues" illustrates the desolate nature of the Tijuana asteroid and contrasts it sharply with the more urban planets and moons we will travel to in future sessions.

Cowboy Bebop's scoring in this episode is reminiscent of *Firefly*. It also resembles the music of *Trigun*, which began airing the same season as *Cowboy Bebop*. *Trigun*'s interpretation of the space western was far more literal than that of *Bebop* and other travel-oriented science fiction. The series, based on a manga by Yasuhiro Nightow (Japanese: Naitō) and adapted by Studio Madhouse, takes place entirely on one planet: Gunsmoke, after the well-known TV western series. As viewers would expect from that name, the planet resembles the American West, filled with cowboys and other gunslingers. Like *Cowboy Bebop*, *Trigun* was popular among American anime fans, likely due to its western aesthetic and plot, as well as its resemblance to American sci-fi.

The *Trigun* soundtrack was composed by Tsuneo Imahori, who is a member of the Seatbelts, Yōko Kanno's band that plays on the *Cowboy Bebop* soundtrack. His music for *Trigun* relies upon a combination of industrial sounds, heavy on percussion and electronic effects, and the more typical scoring of spaghetti western films: acoustic guitars and breathy flutes. The similarity in instrumentation establishes Gunsmoke's "western-ness," but also its futuristic artificiality. The show's backstory is that the planet was settled by human earthling colonists, and there are hints of advanced technology around the edges of the show's late nineteenth-century western aesthetic, such as large robotic machines that transfer people from place to place, or the mysterious plant-like objects that fuel the planet.

Notably, *Trigun*'s world is not only more western but also more rural than that of *Cowboy Bebop*. *Trigun* depicts a more desolate environment—not only literally, since the planet of Gunsmoke is mostly desert, but also figuratively, as even in its early, comedic episodes, all the characters seem to be in constant danger. *Cowboy Bebop* has more heavily populated urban environments, with many people going about their day. Reflecting its environment, the music of *Trigun* is that of the rural American south and west—bluegrass and country—rather than the hip, urban jazz of *Cowboy Bebop*. The *Trigun* soundtrack fuses industrial and acoustic musics, showcasing how the presence of space-age technology contrasts with the Wild West setting.

This relationship between setting and music is a common feature of narrative film music; it is the "narrative cuing" that Claudia Gorbman describes as a key principle of classical film scoring (1987: 73). *Cowboy Bebop* features a greater variety of environments than *Trigun*, so it musically distinguishes them from each other while still keeping a consistent aesthetic for the overall series. Instead of bringing new cues in for each world, however, it reuses the same ones to different degrees; hence it establishes each world's setting in the context of what viewers have already seen, shaping the viewers' feelings with each newly introduced world. Every episode includes some country/folk cues (those with acoustic guitar or harmonica) and some jazzy ones (those with big bands), but the balance between them conveys what kind of planet the characters are visiting.

Case Study #2: "Stray Dog Strut"

In its second session, *Cowboy Bebop* takes pains to distinguish its second world from that of Tijuana. Session 2, "Stray Dog Strut," brings Spike and Jet to Mars, the land of the Tijuana heroine's dreams. The session introduces Ein, the data dog, along with recurring musical themes representing him and

Radical Edward (Ein's human friend), including "Bad Dog No Biscuits" and "Cat Blues." It also uses significantly more jazz and rock cues than "Asteroid Blues," outside of the traditional chase and fight sequences. One notable cue that is first featured in this episode—including in the preview after "Asteroid Blues"—is "Want It All Back," a late 1960s-style blues-rock anthem featuring a female vocalist (Mai Yamane) belting about a deadbeat ex-boyfriend.

"Want It All Back" appears during a frantic chase scene, as Spike and the episode's two sets of criminals—his target, Abdul Hakim, and a group of scientists doing illegal animal research—chase after Ein through the streets of Mars. The lyrics appear to have nothing to do with the scene, but they operate as a reference to the previous session. The vocalist sings, mockingly: "You said you wanted to see Paris / so I took you to the movies / 'Bon Ami' or something French like that." She snidely dismisses her lover's desire to see the world and complains that she spent much money attempting to give him the worldly experiences he wanted. The song refers back to the way that Katerina idealized Mars in the last episode, pointing out that Mars is not what it's cracked up to be. "Stray Dog Strut" is similar to many other cities that are presented in the *Cowboy Bebop* universe; mostly a backdrop for shady crime, it is full of confused people. The rest of the episode's scoring focuses on minor-key, film-noir-style jazz, representing the suspicious characters of both Hakim, the episode's villain, and the planet where he runs and hides. Even though we meet ordinary people on Mars, they're all involved in somewhat underground, suspicious ventures: a headshop cashier, a woman who deals in exotic pets (and dismisses Ein as just another Welsh corgi, not realizing he is a lab-engineered data dog), and a fortune teller who tries to help Hakim. Far from being a promised land, Mars likely would have just led Asimov and his girlfriend back down the same paths they had taken on Tijuana.

"Pierrot le Fou": Music as Atmosphere

Mars is a planet to which *Cowboy Bebop* returns in later episodes. The series depicts Mars through a cozier lens in Spike's memories of the place, where violent gun battles contrast with soft, nostalgic music such as the music-box melody of "Memory" (including in the opening scene of "Asteroid Blues") and the choir-and-piano of "Green Bird" (in his flashback in session 5, "Ballad of Fallen Angels"). These nostalgic settings could reflect that Mars is a diverse planet (it certainly seems to be one of the most populated), or that Spike is a sentimental, unreliable narrator. The latter hypothesis is supported by Spike's episodes, which will be explored further in Chapter 7. Most of the episodes set on Mars, however, reflect the more complicated, less positive vision of "Stray Dog Strut."

Cowboy Bebop takes the darker vision the furthest in session 20, "Pierrot le Fou." The episode, focusing on a mad, childlike serial killer, includes less music and dialogue than most other sessions of *Cowboy Bebop*. The music that is present is extremely effective and unusual to the series, and it coordinates with the striking visual direction (primarily lighting and character movement) to tell the story. Here, too, Mars is depicted as a shady, forbidding place, with the episode taking place on dark alleyways and a creepy abandoned theme park.

Furthermore, "Pierrot le Fou" is a masterful example of world-building and the creation of atmosphere. The concept of atmosphere is not just the literal surroundings of a science-fictional or fantasy world; it often depends just as much on emotional reactions. The atmosphere turns a perfectly safe, tranquil neighborhood during the day into an unsettling place at night, when most of the Mars scenes in the episode take place. This is similar to the Japanese concept of *kūki*, a social atmosphere, or "the atmosphere of a situation to which all are expected to pay heed" (Manabe 2015: 111–12). "Pierrot le Fou" is the series' only example of pure horror; the only other one that comes close is session 11, "Toys in the Attic," but its all-just-a-dream ending undermines the horror and turns it into humor. The "Pierrot" episode achieves this difference in both genre and emotional tone through the visual and musical atmosphere that it creates.

"Pierrot le Fou" largely eschews the musical genre trappings of other *Cowboy Bebop* episodes. When it does use music, it relies on two main devices. The first—a very sparse, dissonant music—occurs in the scenes where the episode's villain, Tongpu (also known as Mad Pierrot), fights Spike and other characters.[3] These works feature sharp, contrasting notes and chords from string and percussion instruments, separated by long periods of silence, or they feature drone-like effects. The sounds resemble the music in the confrontation scenes with Scorpio in *Dirty Harry*, which relies on dissonant, atmospheric chords combined with drone effects and metallic, high-pitched sounds. The tracks used in "Pierrot le Fou" use much longer and more consistent periods of silence than either of those tracks. These moments of silence reinforce the isolation of Tongpu and his victim, and the empty, dark, foreboding nature of their surroundings—the back alleys of Mars at night.

The other major use of music in "Pierrot le Fou" comes in its visually brightest and most disturbing scene: when the audience learns how Tongpu became the mindless, random killer that he is. The music is the Seatbelts' reinterpretation of Pink Floyd's "On the Run," the third track on *Dark Side of the Moon* (1973), with important alterations. Both songs are instrumental works featuring synthesized sequencer repeating a fast-note loop, but the Seatbelts version uses a different set of notes, in a group of twelve instead of eight. In both songs, the sequence varies little across the work in tempo and rhythm, although the notes and the volume change. The most audible changes are the additions of other sounds to the texture, including percussion instruments, electronic effects, and non-musical sounds. It is a drone, static in its constant motion. Sonically the opposite of the music in earlier fight scenes, "On the Run" is noise that never ceases. It is the perfect accompaniment for a blindingly bright scene in an episode filled with darkness and shadows.

The music also fits the narrative content of the scene. As Jet and Ed watch along, viewers learn that Tongpu was an experiment of the ISSP (*Cowboy Bebop*'s police force) to build a perfect assassin. The experiment was discontinued when it was found to have caused a marked regression of Tongpu's mind, leaving him with the mental capacity of a young child but the physical abilities of a lethal assassin. The camera alternates between images of Tongpu as he regresses further and further, and shots of the lab from Tongpu's point of view, focusing on the odd-colored eyes of the lab's resident cat staring at him. Combined with the music, this scene creates a visceral horror; the viewer can feel Tongpu's mounting terror as he is subject to further experiments and his mind regresses. The relentless, cycling notes signify how he is trapped, while the gradual addition of other sounds to the texture gives the music a feeling of escalation, signifying how Tongpu's condition is deteriorating over time. The synthesizer also connects the scene with technology, the source of Tongpu's despair.

"Pierrot le Fou" culminates in Tongpu and Spike's final confrontation at a theme park on Mars. The music here is no different from typical theme park music, but combined with the images of dilapidated-but-still-moving theme park robots it creates an unsettling, disturbing atmosphere. Like "On the Run," fairground music is also mechanical and repetitive, but it is less tied to Tongpu's emotional state. It forms an audiovisual counterpoint, like the use of children's or fairground music in horror films. The setting gives Spike and Tongpu a suitably disturbing final battle scene that also plays on Tongpu's childishness. It is the final cherry on top of the masterful atmosphere of "Pierrot le Fou," which combines visuals and music to maximize the horror in every scene.

Conclusion

One of the more interesting examples of planets that receive sparse scoring is Earth. The characters first visit Earth in session 9, "Jamming with Edward," which, as per the title, introduces Radical Edward (heretofore referred to as "Ed," which is what the characters call her). As with sessions 1 and 2, this comes right after a musically and otherwise aesthetically contrasting session, "Waltz for Venus." "Jamming with Edward" is striking for the relatively few musical cues it uses compared to other episodes. This musical sparseness reflects Earth's emptiness; much of it has been destroyed by the gate accident in the 2010s, and it remains largely uninhabitable (although, as the episode demonstrates, there are still several large human settlements). Earth reappears in session 24, "Hard Luck Woman," that focuses on Faye and Ed's pasts. Once again, it has little music of its own, other than the respective characters' motifs and the music that frames their memories and nostalgia (Chapter 6). Earth is a planet filtered solely through characters' memories. Mars, on the other hand, can be seen both as it is—a bustling, urban planet, with many dark corners—and through Spike's own unreliable narration.

Cowboy Bebop is significantly less world-focused than many other science fiction anime. It focuses largely on its characters' individual emotional journeys and references to other genres of film apart from sci-fi. However, when it turns its sonic lens on its environments, it richly conveys the diversity of places and peoples across its world of the late twenty-first-century solar system. Its aesthetics work together to paint the settings of *Cowboy Bebop* as palpable, engaging, and varied places in which viewers could easily imagine themselves. The music plays no small role in this scene painting.

5 See You, Space Cowboy: Music and Genre Parody in "Cowboy Funk" and "Mushroom Samba"

Referenced Sessions
#17 Mushroom Samba
#22 Cowboy Funk

Referenced External Works
A Fistful of Dollars (1964)
For a Few Dollars More (1965)
The Good, the Bad and the Ugly (1966)
Shaft (1971)
Super Fly (1972)

One of the many ways that *Cowboy Bebop* attempts to "become a new genre itself" is the way in which it engages with existing film genres. Several sessions are parodies of existing films or film genres. For example, session 11, "Toys in the Attic" (Japanese title: "Yamiyo no Hevi Rokku," or "Dark Night of Heavy Rock"), is a mystery about a disease-causing monster that parodies the *Alien* film series (1979–) and *2001: A Space Odyssey* (1968); session 17, "Mushroom Samba," is a goofy episode focused on Ed and Ein which parodies blaxploitation films; and session 22, "Cowboy Funk," which involves Spike's cowboy-themed doppelganger, parodies spaghetti westerns.

In a sense, these three genre parodies represent a fusion of the genres that make up *Cowboy Bebop* itself. The series belongs most obviously to science fiction, revolving around the crew of a spaceship. It also has elements of the gangster film, of which the more urban variety of blaxploitation (where "Mushroom Samba" focuses its parody) could be seen as a subgenre. Lastly, the series is a space western, invoking the tropes of the genre in how its universe treats bounty hunters. The show calls them cowboys and uses western imagery (country music, cowboy hats and boots) in the "Big Shots" show-within-a-show for bounty hunters, announcing new criminals to capture. Bounty hunters are a common character type within westerns, especially the darker, more revisionist westerns that Sergio Leone's spaghetti westerns played such a major part in establishing as a sub-genre.

For the purpose of this chapter, I will focus on "Cowboy Funk" and "Mushroom Samba." Both spaghetti westerns and blaxploitation films make iconic use of particular musical styles; therefore, music is key to a successful parody of either genre. In this chapter, I will explore how *Cowboy Bebop*'s soundtrack for these two sessions references the music of each genre, and the role that music and sound play in their parodies.

From Space Cowboys to Space Samurai: Music in "Cowboy Funk"

The spaghetti western—Italian-made westerns, particularly those from the 1960s–1970s that feature dark, revisionist perspectives—is a ripe genre for parody, particularly in animation.[1] In the sketch-based style of Western animation that experienced resurgence in the 1990s, references to popular films and genres are common. When modern animators want to skewer the western, the easiest target is Sergio Leone's spaghetti westerns. Their dark tones and tropes were so influential that they're more likely to be familiar to modern viewers than the optimistic Hollywood westerns that prevailed before the 1960s.

Additionally, the spaghetti western—especially Leone's *Dollars* Trilogy, starring Clint Eastwood in *A Fistful of Dollars* (1964), *For a Few Dollars More* (1965), and *The Good, the Bad and the Ugly* (1966)—has many well-known tropes that viewers, even those who haven't seen these exact films, will recognize. Such tropes include the mysterious, quiet stranger who wanders into a town from nowhere and leaves a trail of violence in his wake; the relative lack of dialogue; and, especially, the use of music. Ennio Morricone made his reputation composing the scores for westerns by Leone and other directors, and his particular use of instrumentation and tonality gave the films an iconic sound. Particularly memorable are the main themes for each film, heard during the opening credits, and repeated in various forms throughout the film. Animated parodies like *Animaniacs'* "The Good, the Boo, and the Ugly" play the theme with a few notes changed, to establish the show as a parody of spaghetti westerns.[2]

The spaghetti western takes on extra resonance when parodied in anime, given the genre's roots in Japanese film. During the 1960s, North American and European filmmakers re-used the plots of Akira Kurosawa's films, moving their settings to the nineteenth-century American West. For example, *A Fistful of Dollars* takes its story from Kurosawa's *Yojimbo* (1961), while John Sturges's American revisionist western *The Magnificent Seven* (1960) is based on Kurosawa's *Seven Samurai* (1954). Referencing these films in anime completes that circle of cultural exchange. "Cowboy Funk" even references this cycle, when its cowboy character decides to play a samurai and rides past Spike in his new costume at the end of the episode.

"Cowboy Funk" is more than just a riff on spaghetti westerns. The episode features Spike taking down a terrorist bomber who dresses as a Teddy bear and hides his bombs in this costume (hence the name, Teddy Bomber). Spike gets close many times, but he keeps being thwarted by a fellow bounty hunter—Cowboy Andy, a blond, goofy, dim-witted version of Spike. He dresses like a cowboy and even rides a horse to the scene of the crime. Andy is at the center of the riff on the spaghetti western in "Cowboy Funk," both musically and otherwise.

In many respects, Cowboy Andy is a comedic version of the spaghetti western hero. Protagonists in Leone's films, like Clint Eastwood's Man with No Name from the *Dollars* Trilogy, differed from earlier western heroes because of their ambiguous morals. They were drifters riding in from nowhere, killing indiscriminately, and working for money (or the promise of it) rather than for the law. Eastwood's characters often played opposing characters off against each other for his own gain, as in *A Fistful of Dollars*. Bounty hunters were popular choices for protagonists, with their mixture of selfishness and lawfulness. Andy is the comedic parody of all these contradictions. He tries to do the right thing but is thwarted by his own stupidity. He repeatedly accuses Spike and Jet of being the Teddy Bomber, even after the real Teddy Bomber identifies himself. This mistake allows the culprit to escape, and everyone leaves the scene in a pile of bodies and destruction. The scene recalls the violent, destructive endings in spaghetti westerns. In *Cowboy Bebop*, however, the destruction results from Andy's ineptitude rather than from callousness.

The music also shows a strong fidelity to the conventions of the spaghetti western, particularly in the musical characterization of heroes. Other parodies of spaghetti westerns, like the aforementioned *Animaniacs* short, copy the basic structure of one of the films' musical themes (e.g., from *The Good, the Bad and the Ugly*) and alter it just enough to avoid copyright issues while still keeping it recognizable to the audience. *Cowboy Bebop*'s primary theme for the episode, indicated in the second official soundtrack (*Cowboy Bebop Blue*) as "Go Go Cactus Man," represents Morricone's style in broad strokes. It is still recognizable enough to those who've seen Leone's westerns (or absorbed their tropes through pop-cultural osmosis) to recognize it as a reference to those films. The comments on one YouTube upload of the song are filled with references to Leone, Morricone, and Eastwood.[3] Kanno shows how to preserve that stylistic fingerprint without copying an existing theme. She creates a wholly new theme that sounds as if it could have been used for a Leone film.

This kind of composition requires careful attention to Morricone's style, particularly his tonality and orchestration. In his study of music in the *Dollars* Trilogy, Charles Leinberger discusses how Morricone builds his melodies on a signature six-note scale: the Aeolian (natural minor) scale, minus the sixth scale degree (2012: 131–47). He calls this a "minor hexatonic" scale, and it forms the basis of the theme from *A Fistful of Dollars*. Kanno uses this scale in "Go Go Cactus Man." Kanno's melody makes heavy use of the tonic, third, fifth and seventh scale degrees, as though it is spelling out a chord on a guitar; this is similar to the theme from *The Good, the Bad and the Ugly*. In his film score guide to that film, Leinberger also notes Morricone's heavy use of the Dorian mode and the natural minor (Aeolian mode) in his Leone scores.[4] He sees this as a reference to older European music, given the natural minor's heavy use in Celtic music and the Dorian mode's in medieval chant (Leinberger 2004: 27–9). He cites his own interview with Morricone, stating that the composer acknowledged the influence of Celtic music on this aspect of his scoring (Leinberger 2004, 27). All of these elements combine to give Morricone's spaghetti western scores a distinct tonal language, one that composers like Kanno can easily adopt. This tonality is combined with an even more recognizable Morricone stamp—his instrumentation.

Morricone's use of instruments and voices is the most distinctive and imitated part of his Leone scores, and Leinberger discusses many of them in depth. Two of these discussions, on the use of electric guitar and the human voice, are relevant to "Go Go Cactus Man." The electric guitar is an obviously anachronistic choice that connects the old West to the "popular music of the modern American cowboy" (Leinberger 2004: 20). Morricone's innovation was to add a "twangy" sound, reminiscent of California surf music, and other 1960s instrumental rock hits like "Apache" and John Barry's James Bond theme (Leinberger 2004: 20–1). "Go Go Cactus Man" prominently features a low, twangy surf guitar, similar to the ones heard in Morricone themes like the one for *The Good, the Bad and the Ugly*.

Leinberger's discussion of "the human voice as a musical instrument" refers to two Morricone techniques: wordless singing that mimics wind instruments (as featured in the "wah wah" sound of *The Good, the Bad and the Ugly* theme), and the prominent use of the human whistle. In "Go Go Cactus Man," the whistle is the melodic voice. Morricone uses a whistled melody in *A Fistful of Dollars*, where it serves as a leitmotiv for Clint Eastwood's character, often used to announce his arrival in a scene.[5] The whistling is not connected to any particular character; it seems to be a non-diegetic part of the soundtrack. "Cowboy Funk" uses Andy's theme in a similar way but blurs the line between diegesis and nondiegesis, in what Robynn J. Stilwell calls the "fantastical gap" between the two (2007: 184). The characters are aware of the whistling, asking, "Where is that whistling coming from?" After Andy has repeatedly mistaken Spike and his friends for the Teddy Bomber and derailed their attempts to capture the real one, they hear the whistled theme and react with dread. In one moment, Spike even thinks he hears Andy coming, only for it to be another person whistling a different tune. "Cowboy Funk" parodies the use of leitmotivs in Leone's spaghetti westerns in a self-aware, comedic way—one that works even for viewers who are not familiar with the *Dollars* Trilogy, but is extra-amusing for those who are.

Another unusual instrument used in both Morricone's scores and "Go Go Cactus Man" is the jaw harp, also known as the Jew's harp. This instrument is one of the oldest in the world, and is a lamellophone, played by depressing and releasing a metal tongue in front of the open mouth. This gives the jaw harp a sharp, twangy sound. Morricone used it to great effect in *For a Few Dollars More*, which cemented his reputation for unusual instrumentation. In that score, the jaw harp is juxtaposed in contrast to the melodic whistle, as it is also in "Go Go Cactus Man."

The episode goes to great lengths to compare Cowboy Andy to Spike: characters like Faye and Jet go on about how they're basically the same person, although Andy is an exaggeration of Spike's flaws. What the music communicates is how much Andy's cowboy-themed bounty hunter is also a comedic inversion of Eastwood's archetypal character. Andy has the look, and he has the music—a perfect pastiche of the *Dollars'* musical language. What he does not have is the attitude. Where Eastwood's Man with No Name is quiet, Andy is loud, drawing as much attention to himself as possible with his ridiculous antics, such as riding horseback into modern skyscrapers. When Andy captures Faye, she learns that he is a rich boy who has no need to be a bounty hunter, except that he enjoys pretending to be a cowboy. He also loves ridiculous excess in all parts of his life, as Faye notices that his home is full of gaudy, kitschy furniture. Where Eastwood's character represents gritty, harsh authenticity, Andy is goofy and fake.

Spike is actually much closer to the spaghetti western hero than Andy. Spike works mainly for money, without much consideration for the law, and he lives life day-to-day without thinking about the future. Spike is not necessarily quiet, but he is much sneakier than Andy. Spike could be read as an exploration of the Man-with-No-Name character type as an actual character—an attempt to name him and look at how his lifestyle and behavior actually affect him and his psyche. Andy is a naïve, carefree version of Spike, perhaps reflecting what his character may have been without the troubles that plague him in his focus episodes (Chapter 7). In this light, it seems amusing that Andy is trying so hard to be something he is not, and his music reflects this pretention.

Just as "Go Go Cactus Man" shows the ease with which one can put on a costume to play a part, it also easily constructs its own version of a Morricone theme—or rather, several Morricone-like themes into one parody. It is another piece of costume for Andy and another self-conscious reference for the session.

These connections between "Cowboy Funk" and spaghetti westerns resonate with other aspects of the *Cowboy Bebop* series, including music. Leinberger discusses how Morricone uses the same theme with different orchestration as leitmotivs for different characters in *The Good, the Bad and the Ugly*. The *Cowboy Bebop* score often uses a similar technique, taking motifs defined heavily around a particular character (like Jet's "The Singing Sea") and changing the instruments to use them in a different context ("Stella By Moor" in "Waltz for Venus"). This shared technique of theme recycling demonstrates the extent to which the *Dollars* Trilogy influenced *Cowboy Bebop*'s approach to music, beyond the session that parodies spaghetti westerns.

"Cowboy Funk" is the only time in the series that a character (Cowboy Andy) utters the series' signature sign-off, "See you, space cowboy." It is the one time when our characters get to encounter and even play themselves as actual cowboys. (At the end of the episode, Spike dons Andy's cowboy hat after Andy decides to become a samurai.) Like Andy in relation to the spaghetti western hero, and his music in relation to the scoring, perhaps "Cowboy Funk" is a comic exaggeration of the quirks of the entire series.

Music in "Mushroom Samba"

According to Watanabe, the *Cowboy Bebop* staff sometimes "first put in the title and thought about the content later." For "Mushroom Samba," the process was different: "... the title came first. So mushrooms come out in the plot. Out of the songs we'd already gotten, I assembled together those that were funky" (Watanabe, interview). The episode resulting from this unusual process is less rooted in film genre parody than "Cowboy Funk." Watanabe says that "Mushroom Samba" is intended as an "homage to blaxploitation movies of the 1970s, featuring characters like those appearing in *Shaft*"—the first Hollywood blaxploitation film, released in 1971. As with "Cowboy Funk," this homage is largely played out through the episodic characters and soundtrack.[6]

Several of the black characters in "Mushroom Samba" are named for iconic blaxploitation heroes and heroines. Coffee, the female bounty hunter whom Ed and Ein meet first (at 7:23), is named for the titular heroine of *Coffy* (1973), a vigilante played by Pam Grier. She shares Grier's large afro and low-cut shirt. Another character (at 10:01) calls himself one of the "Shaft brothers," and his outfit resembles Priest's iconic suit in *Super Fly* (1972). The subplot centers on a drug dealer, a type common not only in *Cowboy Bebop* sessions but also in blaxploitation films, where they can be both heroes and villains. Though these episodic characters interact with Ed and Ein, they primarily serve as background events to the two main characters' adventures.

The session also references the spaghetti western *Django* (1966), as well as countercultural films of the late 1960s and 1970s. As Ed and Ein find psychedelic mushrooms, and Spike, Jet, and Faye trip after eating them, the desert setting and trippy sequences resemble similar scenes in drug-influenced countercultural films of that period, making the episode seem like a comedic love letter to the independent filmmaking of the era. None the less, blaxploitation is the most obvious influence for "Mushroom Samba" and sets the tone for its soundtrack.

Blaxploitation in film began with the controversial independent release, *Sweet Sweetback's Baadasssss Song* (1971). It was quickly co-opted by the Hollywood mainstream; *Shaft* was released the same year. As the name suggests, the genre featured primarily African-American casts in action/gangster plots or genre fiction (like horror and westerns), centered on urban or southern rural neighborhoods in a sensationalized light. The genre faded away after the 1970s along with other genres of exploitation film. It has continued to influence other film genres, especially action films. Directors like Quentin Tarantino show their genre literacy by referencing blaxploitation icons and tropes. *Cowboy Bebop*'s "Mushroom Samba" is part of this tradition.

Blaxploitation films were among the first to feature soundtracks full of funk—an African-American musical genre associated with the busy bass lines, syncopated horns, and multilayered drum patterns of James Brown, Sly and the Family Stone, and Parliament Funkadelic, among other artists. Often, popular funk artists played on these soundtracks; for example, *Super Fly* had an original soundtrack by Curtis Mayfield. As Richard Dyer describes, this music "claims space for black men" during walking sequences (2013: 158). With funk playing in the background, these characters take up both physical and aural space in the world of the film, with both camera and audio framing them as powerful and prominent. Such multisensory framing, Dyer argues, is less necessary for white protagonists, who are assumed to be the centers of their world and are automatically afforded space. Black protagonists have to make space for themselves.

In the world of *Cowboy Bebop*, the black characters in "Mushroom Samba" are supporting players to Ed and Ein's adventure. None the less, they take up significantly more space than most of the darker-skinned characters in *Cowboy Bebop.*[7] They are the focus of the session's humor and genre commentary, and they interact multiple times with the main characters. Drug dealer Domino's actions drive the session's plot (what little it has), not only because he is the weekly bounty target, but also because his illegal mushrooms affect the other characters. Coffee and Shaft attempt to track him, Ed, and Ein down for messing up their plans, leading to the climactic chase scene that is accompanied by "Mushroom Hunting."

"Mushroom Hunting" is musically similar to "Superfly," the title song of *Super Fly*, among other blaxploitation film songs. Both songs begin with a syncopated bass line before adding other instruments; recalling Archie Bell in "Tighten Up" or Sly Stone in "Dance to the Music," the singer goads the players to join with "Let's kick the beat!" Like "Superfly," they include a mix of talking and singing, with "Mushroom Hunting" leaning more toward talking than "Superfly."[8] Both include prominent rhythm instruments (bass and drums), sparser use of melodic instruments, and they mostly stay on one chord. They both describe dangerous situations. "Superfly" is about a drug dealer, like the protagonist Priest; it depicts the business in a negative, scary, but still cool way, and Priest is shown trying to get out of it. Lastly, both songs are used in the narrative climax of the film or episode (i.e., the chase scene in "Mushroom Samba" and Priest's move to his final deal in *Super Fly*). Neither theme appears at all in their respective works until then, despite being the iconic music in them.

Priest has more driving sequences than walking sequences in *Super Fly*, and Dyer says this disconnects him from the space of the film's action and shows how he lives multiple lives, "separat[ing] the bohemian space of his white (Greenwich Village?) girlfriend's apartment from the space of his business" (2013: 157). The music is also more melodious and disconnected from Priest's persona compared with the themes in *Shaft* to its title character. For example, Curtis Mayfield's soft falsetto is very different from Priest's deep, commanding baritone.

In the interview conducted for this book, Shinichirō Watanabe specifically mentioned *Shaft* as a blaxploitation film that influenced the music of "Mushroom Samba." While the sonic similarities were less obvious to me than those of *Super Fly*, *Shaft* also includes a number of vocal funk songs at pivotal moments, including the characters' walk to the scene of the film's climactic moment (rescuing a drug dealer's daughter from a kidnapping).

"Mushroom Hunting" is the only example of funk in *Cowboy Bebop*'s soundtrack. Like "Go Go Cactus Man," "Mushroom Samba" is a homage to a genre that the other episodes' soundtracks merely hint at or borrow elements from in the service of a different type of music. *Cowboy Bebop*'s musical world intersects with an entirely different one for a brief moment. This brevity of contact reinforces the feeling that "Mushroom Samba" is a comic-relief episode that is disconnected from the larger, tragic narrative of the series.

The explicit genre reference also reinforces Ed and Ein's position as outsiders in this episode. While they involve themselves in Domino's conflicts with Shaft and Coffee, they do so as a meddling kid and her dog who do not really understand these characters' problems or lives. Their innocence causes problems, which provides the humor. In the "Mushroom Hunting" chase sequence, Ed and Ein appear as goofballs having a laugh as they race through the other characters' tense stand-off. By contrast, Ed is surprisingly clever throughout the other half of the episode, where she tests the "bad mushrooms" on Spike, Jet, and Faye. Ed sees Ein start bouncing around oddly after eating one of Domino's mushrooms, realizes that they are a drug, and decides to test this hypothesis by seeing how they affect the rest of the crew. The music reinforces Ed and Ein as connected to and understanding the world of the *Bebop* crew, by using more traditional musical choices for those moments. They are also shown as being blissfully unaware of the problems of the larger world, and their actions involving the black characters reinforce their difference and separation from that world. "Mushroom Hunting" is the incursion of another film genre entirely into the *Bebop* world, and it reinforces Ed and Ein's separation from that other world.

Another musical sequence, "Chicken Bone," disputes their isolation. The music is used for a scene in which Ed and Ein bounce across the desert, mastering their landscape—a more direct conquering of space than the walking scenes from blaxploitation films that Dyer describes. In blaxploitation walking scenes, the camera zooms out to show the protagonists embedded in dense urban environments. "Chicken Bone" seems to speak for Ed and Ein, using a high, childlike voice repeating nonsense lyrics about how "I like, you like, he likes, she likes chicken bone" and cooking instructions for the titular bone ("roast it well with Cajun sauce … bake it well with Asian sauce … It's good for your healthy life"). The vocal style resembles that of Ed and Ein's other musical themes (Chapter 6).

"Chicken Bone" uses many electronic beats and sound effects, closer to techno-influenced varieties of funk of the 1980s rather than the 1970s styles heard in blaxploitation. Like both versions of funk, the track is highly rhythmic and danceable, as Ed demonstrates by skipping along to its rhythm. The music draws Ed and Ein into the musical soundscape of "Mushroom Samba" by finding a middle ground between the irreverent poppy sounds of their music and that of the episode. These disparate elements are merged into a cohesive whole in a scene where these characters demonstrate a mastery of their environment.

While "Mushroom Hunting" is an outlier in the *Bebop* soundtrack, it foreshadows developments in Watanabe's career. Later works like *Samurai Champloo* and especially *Space Dandy* use funk music and related genres more extensively. Overall, both of the genre parody sessions in *Cowboy Bebop* demonstrate Watanabe and Kanno's strong awareness of musical genre, and how it is used to create certain expectations in film. This would become a strong thread not only throughout their other works together and apart (as discussed in Chapters 1 and 2), but also in *Cowboy Bebop*'s own success. The series is renowned for the ways in which it refreshes the familiar by finding innovative approaches to genres and mixing their elements. This freshness is the key by which *Bebop* becomes "a new genre itself."

6 Jamming with Edward (and Jet and Faye): Scoring *Bebop*'s Characters

Referenced Sessions
#3 Honky Tonk Women
#9 Jamming with Edward
#10 Ganymede Elegy
#15 My Funny Valentine
#16 Black Dog Serenade
#18 Speak like a Child
#24 Hard Luck Woman

At first glance, the cast of *Cowboy Bebop* can feel simple and stereotypical. Many viewers walk away unable to articulate why they care about these characters so much; I certainly felt this way on my first viewing. Each character receives only a few episodes to tell viewers who they are, where they came from, and where they are going. None the less, *Cowboy Bebop* wrings rich stories out of these small pieces of character development. Beneath the character types and episodic adventures lies powerful commentary on the human condition, including gender roles, nostalgia, and memory, and the ways that people forge and destroy relationships. As much as critics and fans highlight the show's references and aesthetics, it is the characters whose stories it tells that keep fans returning to the series.

Kanno's score typically deals in broad strokes, illustrating change through genre rather than the development of thematic motifs. With characters, however, Kanno returns to the familiar film score techniques. She gives each of the main characters (with one major exception) specific, repeating, and varying musical themes that follow him or her through individual focus episodes. In addition, Kanno writes separate music for each character's moments of catharsis, usually with lyrics that express the character's feelings or personality. This chapter examines the music that illustrates each character and discusses the ways in which it makes their stories more emotionally compelling.

Because Chapter 7 focuses on Spike's journey, the present chapter is dedicated to the other members of the *Bebop* crew: Jet Black, Faye Valentine, Radical Ed (and her many other names), and Ein the Data Dog.

Jet Black: The Singing Sea

Jet Black is the gruff old man of the *Bebop*. Spike is already his partner when the story begins in "Asteroid Blues" (session 1), but it was Jet's ship first. He acts as a father figure to the other characters, making their meals and taking up domestic hobbies like bonsai cutting. He also mediates between Spike and Faye, if he bothers with their arguments at all. (When Faye first joins the crew in session 4, "Gateway Shuffle," Jet responds to Spike's anger by repeating, "I don't know, and I have no opinion.") However, he is not emotionless; Jet is as fiercely stubborn as the rest of the characters. He clings to traditional values, such as gender roles. Along with explaining Faye's and other women's behavior with generalizations like "women are too emotional," Jet also subscribes to his own masculine code of honor—what his crew calls his "sense of justice and duty." His nickname is Black Dog, because "when he bites, he won't let go."

Jet's convictions are tested as the series lays out his backstory. *Cowboy Bebop* reveals it piece by piece in "Ganymede Elegy" (session 10) and in "Black Dog Serenade" (session 16). Unlike Faye and Spike, who previously lived outside of the law as a con woman and a hit man respectively, Jet once enforced it. He was a member of the ISSP, the interplanetary future's police system. How and why he left that life, as well as his regrets about it, form the core of Jet's story.

The three main players of *Cowboy Bebop* all start at different life moments. Faye's is just beginning, her memory wiped clean, even if making sense of that forgotten past is the only way she can begin to work toward a new life. Spike's begins *in medias res*; he is atoning for an earlier chapter of his life, and others know he would be better off if he were less obsessed with that past. Jet calls himself an old-timer whose ways are too old-fashioned for the new world. Jet also has the most defined musical stamp, present in several easily recognizable variations throughout his focus episodes.

We first hear Jet's theme as the ballad, "The Singing Sea," sung by Tulivu-Donna Cumberbatch in an expressive cabaret style. It plays as Jet reconnects with old flame Alisa in "Ganymede Elegy." In his other episodes (primarily session 16, "Black Dog

Serenade"), the melody is reworked into two sparser instrumental arrangements that retain the stylistic character of the original: "Farewell Blues," a jazz quartet (muted trumpet, piano, bass, and drums) and "Cosmos," a trumpet solo. A music-box arrangement of the tune, called "Stella By Moor," changes the character of the melody completely, lending it the mystery and nostalgia of Spike's "Memory." This version is the only one not associated with a focus episode for Jet; it defines the character Stella in session 8, "Waltz for Venus." As discussed in Chapter 3, *Cowboy Bebop* frames the blues as the music of authenticity, age, and world-weariness—as "old timers," in Jet's language. Still, the childlike nature of "The Singing Sea" makes it appropriate for preservation in a music box.

"The Singing Sea" is full of nursery-rhyme metaphors and contradictions. The first verse describes the sea and trees as "silent in a noisy way," followed by "the stars are bright / but give no light." The second verse mentions a "checkered cat," along with a "rainbow rat" and a mouse who is "pleased / the moon is cheese." The lyrics are confusing, contrasting with the mournful musical features. Even so, the tonal center moves from A minor to C major, and, on this contrasting mood, the first verse reveals its most serious line: "The world spins backwards every day." Jet's signature song speaks of innocence lost, in a completely different way from a song like "Flying Teapot" (discussed below, in Faye's section). It also suggests a lingering investment in that innocence, as Jet clings to his past. This is why the vocal version debuts in "Ganymede Elegy," the episode most connected to Jet's obsession with reliving and fixing his past mistakes.

Ganymede is Jet's home, and when the *Bebop* lands there to turn in their latest bounty, he finds himself seeking out his old flame, Alisa. "The Singing Sea" plays as the two catch up in her bar. Jet insists she explain why she left him, leaving him nothing but the scrawled word "Farewell." The camera cuts between close-ups of Alisa and overhead shots, suggesting that Jet cannot stop focusing on Alisa—remaining invested in their past relationship—even as he tries to hide it. Alisa serves Jet another reminder of how much he is stuck in the past, suggesting he believes time stands still on Ganymede when he is not there. In fact, years have gone by and much has changed, including Alisa. The affair may be recent in Jet's long memory, but for her—much younger than Jet—it is a "story from long ago." "The Singing Sea" accurately projects Jet's contradictions: not only longing for a more innocent past, but assuming others remain frozen in it, while he still moves through the world and gathers more world-weariness. The scene, and the music, ends when Alisa leaves abruptly, insisting on remaining with current boyfriend Rhint.

Alisa's decision poses problems later on, as Rhint has a bounty on his head. Jet insists to Spike that he handles this matter on his own, and he chases the couple through the Ganymede harbor. Alisa uses the chase to prove her loyalty to Rhint: she shoots at Jet's line when he hooks their boat. Later, she points a gun at him after he has cornered her on land. In that moment, Alisa spells out the old-fashioned, infantilizing ideas that Jet clings to about her: he insists on protecting and leading her, rather than letting her find her own path. She left him because she needed to be free, and for the same reason she refuses to take him back. Jet gradually accepts defeat; even after the police corner Rhint and take him away, he acknowledges that Alisa was right. When she says she will pass the time waiting for Rhint at her bar, Jet responds, "I don't think you'll be waiting for long, because time never stands still."

Before they reach that conclusion, however, *Cowboy Bebop*

has another musical surprise in store in "ELM." This cue is originally heard in the first session, "Asteroid Blues," to signify Katerina's vain hope to live on Mars. "ELM" is an emotional-climax cue that diverges stylistically from the rest of the *Cowboy Bebop* score. It features a tenor vocalist with a guitar in Dorian mode, making it reminiscent of English folk revival. It is wistful but also playful, with the singer voicing the syllables "da" and "la" rather than actual words. "ELM" is reprised during the final moments of Jet and Rhint's chase scene, right before Alisa looks at her former beau and shoots—finally cutting her line to Jet and his restrictive roles. When taken together with its earlier use in "Asteroid Blues," it is fascinating how Katerina and Jet are two different kinds of doomed dreamers: one is defeated by death, the other by resignation and cynicism. "ELM" seems to be the theme for unattainable dreams.

Both "The Singing Sea" and "ELM" fade away or are masked by other sounds by the time they finish playing in the episode. These features suggest incompleteness—how unprepared Jet was to move on from Alisa compared to other parts of his past. Resolution, or lack thereof, plays an even more prominent role in the scoring of Jet's next episode, "Black Dog Serenade."

"Black Dog Serenade" follows Jet's other major regret: how he lost his arm. He was set up by a member of the Syndicate (a major crime organization in the show's world) when trying to catch a crook. Jet relishes the opportunity for revenge, and he finally gets it when an old cop buddy Fad tells him the offender—a sinister boss named Udai—has hijacked a prison transport ship. There is a bounty, plus Jet's own score to settle. Two variations on "The Singing Sea" play key roles in piecing it together: "Cosmos," a shorter version for solo saxophone, and "Farewell Blues," a longer version where the saxophone is accompanied by piano, bass, and drums. "Farewell Blues" also trades melodic material between the saxophone and the piano.

"Cosmos" plays during Jet's flashback to the day he lost his arm. Unlike other characters' more colorful flashbacks (such as Faye's), Jet's memory works like Spike's, in black-and-white, full of shadows and implications but few answers. This first flashback shows us when he finds Udai but stops before Jet loses his arm—when he figures it out and yells, "It's a set-up!" It ends abruptly, before the last two bars of the melody and its harmonic resolution.

Later, we learn the complete truth of Jet's past. He corners Udai in the episode's climax. However, Udai reveals he was not the person who destroyed Jet's arm. It was his old police partner, Fad, betraying him to the Syndicate. As we see the full flashback, we finally hear "Cosmos" in full. It reinforces not only the story's resolution but also Jet's catharsis. He finally knows what he really needs to do, now that he has been forced to face the truth.

This revelation leads to a confrontation with Fad. He admits guilt, resulting in another shoot-off; Jet wins. As Fad lies dying, he asks for a cigarette—recalling an earlier scene in which he lies to Jet that he has quit smoking—and we hear the fully orchestrated "Farewell Blues," but only the final phrase. The song has truly ended, and Jet can make peace and move on with his life. In a time gone by, Fad had promised Jet that, after this mission, they could rejoin the ISSP together. Now, Jet accepts that chapter of his life is truly over.

By the end of "Black Dog Serenade," Jet seems to have come to terms with his mistakes. He is able to move forward in the series into his new life, rather than endlessly reliving those troubles in the way that Faye and especially Spike do. His music reflects his old-fashioned nature and his sorrow, but it reaches a harmonic conclusion—in the more optimistic-sounding relative major—to demonstrate how Jet can truly let go.

Faye Valentine: Flying Teapot

After Spike, Faye Valentine is easily *Cowboy Bebop*'s best-known character. She is iconic as a sexy fanservice character, especially among North American anime fans, for whom *Cowboy Bebop* is often an introduction to anime (or at least, to more adult-oriented anime after being raised on children's series like *Pokémon*).[1] Nearly two decades after *Cowboy Bebop* was first released, Faye's revealing (but not outrageous) outfit remains a cosplay favorite at conventions. Her status as a sex symbol eclipses her role in the series itself.

Her status among fans makes it all the more interesting that Faye does not really have memories of her own. Faye is an amnesiac, and what past she has is too distant to leave many records for her to check. Still, her search for her past and the challenges it poses to our original notions about Faye become her story in the four sessions that highlight her: "Honky Tonk Women" (session 3), "My Funny Valentine" (session 15), "Speak like a Child" (session 18) and "Hard Luck Woman" (session 24). The first merely alludes to her past as being mysterious—Faye tells Spike a tall tale about being "a Romani," and therefore "unable to stay in one place"—while the latter episodes reveal the truth, or at least Faye's best guess of it.

Faye is a fascinating character from a feminist perspective. Her story mirrors the conception of sex symbols as blank slates for viewer projection. She is also defined as a foil for Spike, who refuses to escape his past and describes it as a "dream he never wakes up from." He is defined by his insistence on coming to terms with his past, even if he damages his future prospects, and his careless, easy-come, easy-go philosophy originates from his sense that he has already destroyed them. On the other hand, Faye exhibits similar behavior because she has no past to ground her. When she finds something or someone to fill that need, it always turns out to be a lie. Faye and Spike find this connection in "My Funny Valentine," when she unintentionally reveals her backstory to him and he rejects it. Faye says to a brooding Spike, "At least you have a past." Spike returns, "You have a future. That's what matters."

In regards to musical themes for characters, Faye is a major exception. Every other main character in *Cowboy Bebop* receives at least one repeating musical motif connected with their personalities, backstories, and their relationships with them. Spike gets "Memory"; Jet has "The Singing Sea"; and Ed and Ein have a constellation of shared cues with cat-and-dog titles. Even single-episode characters have their own theme songs, such as "Space Lion" for Gren (in "Jupiter Jazz," Chapter 7) and "Go Go Cactus Man" for Cowboy Andy (Chapter 5). Faye Valentine has no such theme song or motif. What musical moments she has do not recur, existing to illustrate a moment in her life rather than Faye herself. It is a fitting musical characterization for the woman with no past or permanent identity. Faye lacks a musical fingerprint, just as she lacks memories of her past. This motivic lack reflects her unstable, fragile identity. However, music still plays as key a role in Faye's story as it does for every other character in *Cowboy Bebop*.

Faye is introduced in *Cowboy Bebop*'s third episode, "Honky Tonk Women." Her first appearance does little to indicate that Faye will become a more frequent presence in the story, other than Spike's fascination with her. Through a failed con involving a mysterious poker chip, Faye is established as fickle and mysterious, but very unlucky. One of the first things we learn about her is her long list of debts, which the poker-chip gambit is designed to pay off. The debts continue to haunt her throughout the series; her backstory in "My Funny Valentine" explains both Faye's origins and the source of her debts.

In the first scene, Faye attempts to rob an herbal medicine store. After being caught, Faye is questioned by a mob boss accusing her of being "Poker Alice," an infamous con-woman. The scene foreshadows Faye's later revelations when she points out that she cannot be Alice, because Alice would be over 200 years old. The music of this scene evolves out of a riff on electric bass, in minor mode with a flat V. As the scene plays, more and more instruments join the texture, including low, breathy flutes and a muted trumpet. Among the diversity of jazz styles in *Cowboy Bebop*, this cue is associated with film noir. It establishes Faye as mysterious and, in that moment, desperate: she is tied up as the mobster feels up her leg. However, Faye is not a victim: she snarks back at him and hides cards in her short shorts. She turns the tables on the gangsters later in the episode, keeping the money. The message is that Faye is a fast woman with many tricks up her sleeve, who is difficult to understand.

The musical texture of film noir continues throughout this episode, particularly in the scenes centered on Faye. The diegetic music inside the casino, where she first meets Spike, focuses on the sensual; a female vocalist dramatically sighs instead of singing. The overall texture reinforces the idea of Faye as mysterious, cunning, and sexy, but little beyond that as of yet. Many holes are left in the enigma of Faye, and even after she joins the *Bebop* crew and becomes a regular part of the show, they remain unexplained for the next eight episodes. The change comes with her second focus episode, "My Funny Valentine"—and once again, music plays a key role in fleshing out her character.

"My Funny Valentine" consists of Faye's flashbacks to her earliest memories. Faye has just awoken from cryogenic sleep. She meets doctors and a man claiming to be her "lawyer," one Whitney Hagas Matsumoto. He informs Faye that she slept for 54 years, since an accident damaged her body too severely for her era's medical cures. The scene of Faye and Whitney's first meeting begins in a tranquil green forest outside the hospital, accompanied by a piano arrangement of Spike's flashback/nostalgia motif, "Memory." Even Faye's memories are set to someone else's music.

As we watch Faye and Whitney's relationship develop, we hear the episode's musical standout: "Flying Teapot." It accompanies a montage of Whitney introducing Faye to her brave new world: traveling, eating fancy food, and ballroom dancing. "Flying Teapot" stands out against not only the music of Faye's other episodes, but the *Cowboy Bebop* soundtrack as a whole. Instead of jazz, blues, or roots-rock, "Flying Teapot" draws from folk-pop: specifically, that of 1970s singer-songwriters like Joni Mitchell.

"Flying Teapot" features simple instrumentation—vocals and piano, with the occasional interjection of other instruments like saxophones—but uses uneven poetic meter and fleeting tonicizations, giving the song an unsteady feeling. Other distinctive musical gestures include the use of arpeggios with changes in timbre at the top note, as well as the solo female voice that frequently jumps throughout a large range. These gestures resemble Joni Mitchell's style in the 1970s on albums such as *For the Roses* (1972) and *Court and Spark* (1974). Also notable is the sudden harmonization in lower fourths, after a solo vocal line, in "Lay your heart, lay your soul" in "Flying Teapot." These notes are lower in the singer's vocal range than the previous section, with a breathy texture. They sound surprising after the lighter, playful vocal sound in the rest of the song. These techniques—harmonizations in fourths, sudden changes in vocal timbre, and dramatic jumps in register—are those that Joni Mitchell often uses.

The lyrics are also thematically similar to songs by Mitchell and other singer-songwriters of that era. With the death of the 1960s counterculture and its transition into a less starry-eyed outlook, many musicians switched their lyrical focus to personal, confessional lyrics. They often focused on loss of innocence and world-weariness. These themes were all common in Mitchell's music of the 1960s and 70s, including her early hits (e.g., "Both Sides Now," 1967, and "Big Yellow Taxi," 1970). Singer-songwriters of the early 1970s also frequently mentioned travel, furthering the image of the singer as a man or woman of the world. "Flying Teapot" fits both of these tendencies: The singer expresses a frustration with the way her life has not lived up to her dreams ("Sometimes I feel / Oh yes, I could do everything I wanted / And it makes me cry"), including giving up on love ("There's nothing you can do / 'Cause love's such a joke"). Likewise, she talks about travel to Venus with the same casual manner in which Mitchell sings about Amsterdam or Rome ("Carey," 1971): "Now we are flying / To Venus just to kill some time for tea."[2] The song is the *Cowboy Bebop* world's version of that music.

In my interview, the singer, Emily Bindiger, called the song "one of the most playful, fun songs I've ever sung." She also said that its unusual vocals were difficult: "It was really hard, because it kept going straight across what I call my vocal break, and putting me into a soprano range." This alternation between the head and chest voices is characteristic of Joni Mitchell's style. "[Kanno] liked that playfulness of it, so I tried to convey what she was looking for."

What does this combination of Joni Mitchell-like musical techniques and confessional lyrics say about Faye? Later in the episode, we find out that Whitney was lying to her. With the collapse of Earth's gateway destroying all records prior to 2022 (and therefore from 2014, when Faye was frozen), no one really knows why she was preserved or anything about her previous life. Whitney also saddles Faye with his debts when (she believes) he dies, adding to her existing pile, but he turns out to be very much alive, when Jet catches him as the latest bounty target. Whitney is a con man, and his betrayal is the first blow against Faye's innocence. "Flying Teapot"—a title which reflects Faye's beauty and fragility, and the inevitability of her break—is in the voice of the older Faye, commenting on her naïve former self. With the few memories she does have, Faye looks at life from both sides now.

Faye finally gets a real glimpse at her past in "Speak like a Child," after a Betamax tape and player are unexpectedly delivered to their ship. It shows a teenage Faye recording a message for her future self, cheering on whoever she may become. There is little music in this episode that is relevant to Faye, except for a quiet, sparse piano ballad that grows out of the end of the videotape, adding a touch of poignancy to the scene. Her facial reaction shows that this video is meaningful and transformative for her. The music further associates Faye with the piano, and the ballad has some similarities to "Flying Teapot." In her final session, Faye's musical signature changes further.

Coming six episodes later, "Hard Luck Woman" starts right where "Speak like a Child" leaves off. It begins with Faye re-watching the tape, hoping to identify the filmed location and making plans to find it on Earth. She finds not only her old high school but also a now-elderly former classmate. Faye refuses this chance to reconnect, dismissing herself as an "old ghost" and walking away when the classmate's granddaughter enters the scene. Faye clearly regrets her choice later in the episode, as she circles the school's ruins trying to make something out of this experience. Even with her memories returning mid-episode, Faye does not know what to make of her past—and therefore, how to forge it into a foundation for her identity.

This scene culminates in "Call Me Call Me," a rock ballad sung by Steve Conte during the episode's emotional climax. As the title implies, the song is a call for help and connection. It looms over the entire *Cowboy Bebop* cast, alluding to the ways in which Spike and Jet are similarly obsessed with their pasts and reject newer relationships as they cling to old baggage. Faye should be the freest from this baggage, but even she insists on capturing the past she does not remember. Only Ed, as a child (and thus, with all of life ahead of her), gets an answer to the call of the song: as she leaves the *Bebop*, Ein insists on coming with her. Ed has someone to join her as she journeys through life and ponders its questions. Meanwhile, Faye sits in the ruins, searching for her own purpose while rejecting connections with others.

Faye only has a few moments to tell us who she is, moments which are filled with as many questions as answers. This ambiguity includes musical moments; Faye lacks a sonic signature of her own, but makes something interesting out of the sounds that she stumbles across. She is a reflection of *Cowboy Bebop*'s less-is-more philosophy to character writing and the ways in which music is carefully selected to illustrate those moments.

Ed and Ein: Cats (and Dogs) on Mars

Spike, Jet, and Faye's stories are stories of regret, longing, and distorted memories. Luckily, the *Bebop* crew includes two characters of comic relief: Radical Ed, the genius girl hacker, and Ein, the data dog. Though Ed technically has an origin story, it receives little focus and only comes in her final appearance, "Hard Luck Woman"—an episode defined by Faye's story and music. Ein, being an animal, does not have a very complex background at all; his only distinguishing feature is that he seems to be more intelligent than average dogs. In terms of analyzing their music and their functions in the story, Ed and Ein are best understood in their role as comic relief.

Ein is the first new character to join the *Bebop*, in session 2, "Stray Dog Strut." Ed joins in session 9, "Jamming with Edward," carefully placed between two serious, contemplative sessions. Ed and Ein also form the core of "Mushroom Samba" (Chapter 5) and share the spotlight with Faye in "Hard Luck Woman," when they leave the ship together. Ed gets an additional focus episode in "Bohemian Rhapsody" (session 14), in which she saves the crew by defeating a chess mastermind.

That being said, Ed and Ein's music does not necessitate an episode-by-episode analysis. As the show's comic relief, their memorable moments come in interrupting other stories. For example, in one of the first scenes of "Ganymede Elegy," Ed taunts the crew's tied-up bounty target by growling at him, climbing on him, and biting him. The goofy girl and dog provide levity both for other characters and for the audience. They are essentially the ship's mascots. Ein is an animal, and, as the scene in "Ganymede Elegy" demonstrates, Ed often acts like one. In addition, Ed's character design stands out from the rest of the characters: androgynous, with wild, spiky hair that would fit well in other anime, but contrasts with *Cowboy Bebop*'s naturalistic style. She introduces herself with the lengthy, eccentric name she picked out: Edward Wong Hau Pepulu Tivrusky IV. This name is male, includes a mix of nationalities, and finishes with a title, as if Ed were proclaiming herself as royalty. She also speaks in riddles and does her hacking on a computer full of cartoonish smiley faces. Ed flouts social conventions but with a capricious lack of commitment. Ed is the least human and the most animalistic or cartoonish of *Cowboy Bebop*'s human characters. Her music reveals that Ed is an animal—the "cat" to Ein's dog.

Since Ed and Ein are constantly together, their musical themes can best be described together. The titles of the cues on the soundtrack indicate which themes go with which character. Ein's cues are titled after dogs ("Bad Dog No Biscuit"), while Ed's are about cats ("Cat Blues" and "Cats on Mars," a likely reference to David Bowie). The two also share other humorous, childlike, or lighthearted themes, like "Chicken Bone" and "Wo Qui Non Coin." Though these cues show up in other contexts in *Cowboy Bebop*, they are primarily associated with Ed and Ein, and are stylistically similar to their individual themes.

These motifs tend toward artificiality (e.g., electronic effects), simplicity (ostinato patterns, or repeated rhythms), and eccentricity (nonsense language). One example is "Cats on Mars," Ed's theme that is first heard in her introduction episode, "Jamming with Edward." It is associated with Ed's more bizarre, antisocial, and catlike behaviors. It is first heard in a scene in which Ed attempts to connect emotionally with a computer, part of a satellite that traces strange patterns on the Earth's surface. It reveals to Ed its lonely, wistful soul. (In *Cowboy Bebop*, even machines feel regret and nostalgia.) "Cats on Mars" is heard again at the end of the episode after Ed joins the crew; as the Earth turns, we see that the rogue satellite has drawn Ed's face over South America. The drawing not only symbolizes Ed's connection to this machine but also suggests that Ed may have tampered with the Bebop's mission to stop the satellite by keeping it alive or taking it over in its final moments. Perhaps the satellite's personality was all in Ed's mind in the first place; it never communicates to anyone but her. "Cats on Mars" tells us that Ed is smart, mischievous, and above all, unpredictable—just like the cats of its title.

"Cats on Mars" includes lyrics from Yōko Kanno's personal language of nonsense syllables. The most prominent use of that language in the series is "Green Bird," the cue that plays during Spike's montage of his past in "Ballad of Fallen Angels" (Chapter 7). Featuring a choir (with all voices sung by Kanno) and piano, it supports a sad scene filled with Spike's regrets. The two tracks differ in instrumentation. "Cats on Mars" is supported by high-pitched electronic sounds, resembling early video game soundtracks, in a fast ostinato. The singer joins with the same melody. It suggests novelty and playfulness, which is fitting with Ed's personality and her association with technology (through her computer). "Green Bird" uses a chorus in a round, suggesting something much older, and when combined with the visual imagery, far more serious.

Ed and Ein's music shows a resemblance to Shibuya-*kei*, a style of pop music that arose in Japan in the 1990s and included artists such as Cornelius and Flipper's Guitar. Shibuya-*kei* was heavily influenced by 1960s pop, particularly the French *yé-yé* music of Serge Gainsbourg, Brazilian bossa nova, and the *Pet-Sounds*-era Beach Boys (Roberts 2013). Focused on celebrating the kitschier elements of 1960s pop culture, it was often playful and irreverent, like Ed and Ein's music. The similarity to Shibuya-*kei* reflects not only Watanabe's love of it but also the inherent playfulness of the style, the ethos of which seems fitting for these playful characters. "Wo Qui Non Coin" and "Cats on Mars" have the texture of Shibuya-*kei* and a bossa nova-like groove, along with French-sounding nonsense language.

Instead of receiving their own detailed pasts, Ed and Ein live in the moment. In a story in which the characters are defined by their tragic pasts, the laughter and smiles come from the two youngest characters.

Conclusion

The music of *Cowboy Bebop* enhances its narrative, allowing a few quick shots or lines to convey an affective story. Faye and Jet often fail to communicate their feelings in dialogue, and the music expresses what they cannot say and what the visuals can only partially communicate. Music gives voice to the feelings of an older Faye during a montage from her past, or Jet's gradual acceptance of how he lost his arm. For Ed and Ein, music enhances their roles in comic relief, while keeping them connected to the rest of the series. Yōko Kanno gives each character his or her own voice, revealing their hidden depths before the visual or verbal narrative does.

Faye Valentine's lack of a musical theme suggests her lack of a coherent identity. Instead, the music communicates her feelings about her limited past and her search for a longer one through musical genre conventions. Jet Black's themes transform as he learns the facts and processes his feelings about his past. Ed's music puts her eccentricities under a microscope. In Chapter 7, I will explore the role of music in the life of the series' protagonist, Spike Spiegel, including his own complex relationship with his past. For every character aboard the *Bebop*, music is the map to a personal journey.

7 "Ballad of Fallen Angels": Spike Spiegel's Musical Journey

Referenced Sessions
#5 Ballad of Fallen Angels
#12 Jupiter Jazz (Part 1)
#13 Jupiter Jazz (Part 2)
#25 The Real Folk Blues (Part 1)
#26 The Real Folk Blues (Part 2)

The vast majority of *Cowboy Bebop*'s sessions are stand-alone episodes. This makes it unique among anime series, a medium that tends to embrace ongoing plot arcs, even in comedies and other genres that are usually more episodic on American television. None the less, *Cowboy Bebop* remains consistent in character arcs and themes. Five episodes comprise the main plot of the series: "Ballad of Fallen Angels" (session 5), "Jupiter Jazz" parts 1 and 2 (12 and 13), and the finale, "The Real Folk Blues," parts 1 and 2 (25 and 26). These episodes focus on Spike Spiegel, the primary protagonist of the series.

Several episodes (including the premiere, "Asteroid Blues," and session 6, "Sympathy for the Devil") establish key aspects of Spike's character or foreshadow the plot of these five focus episodes. "Pierrot le Fou" showcases an aspect of Spike's appearance that becomes important in the two-part series finale—Spike's eyes have different colors. Together, his five focus episodes form a comprehensible story for Spike, and his relationships with Vicious, his primary antagonist, and Julia, Spike's love interest. Two of Spike's episodes—the "Jupiter Jazz" pair—spend most of the plot with the one-off character Gren rather than Spike, who is absent in many scenes. Still, "Jupiter Jazz" reveals an important part of Spike's backstory and feelings, and Gren's story both parallels and foreshadows Spike's. These five "Spike episodes" form the heart of *Cowboy Bebop*, and their internal plot trajectories and characterizations stand apart from the rest of the series. We rarely hear about Julia in the other 21 sessions, but she's a core element in Spike's five-episode story, even though she doesn't appear until near the end.

This internal logic extends to the use of music in these episodes. Clear patterns among these five sessions help tie together Spike's story, character development, and thematic threads. For example, a few major musical moments dominate these five sessions, with music that is stylistically different. Few of the cues have been used elsewhere in the series. These episodes include some of the most memorable uses of music in the series, the ones most frequently discussed by fans of *Cowboy Bebop*. This unique structure, as well as these sessions' central place in the story, merits its own chapter to discuss why the music in these five sessions is moving, and how these choices affected the reception of Spike's story.

This chapter will also focus on Spike and his musical characterization. It will also examine the musical depictions of the other characters in these five sessions—Vicious, Julia, and

Gren. These characters are also preoccupied with memories to varying degrees, and music again plays a role in establishing nostalgia and fixation with the past.

The Unbearable Lightness of Being Spike Spiegel

Spike is introduced as someone who seems not to have a care in the world. He is defined by phrases, both in his own dialogue and in the sign-off captions at the end of episodes, like "easy come, easy go." He embodies what Milan Kundera might call the lightness of being—trying to avoid attachments, choosing a nomadic lifestyle in order to do so, and often expressing disdain for his shipmates.[1] After Ed joins the ship, Spike announces that the three things he hates are "kids, animals and women with attitudes." Spike might just be irritated by Faye, Ed, and Ein. Still, he defines them in that moment—"women, children, and pets"—in a way that encapsulates the emotional ties of love and family.

The lightness of Spike's life is a façade. Kundera's novel suggests that the light approach to life is unsustainable (or unbearable), and that we all inevitably have some heaviness that pins us to a certain part of the world. This is the case for Spike as well, and the show slowly lets this past creep in around its edges. As early as session 1, we see flashbacks to Spike's former life, with the mysterious rainy alley and the rose that drops in it, the only bit of color in this black-and-white world. The music clearly signals the importance of this scene: the music-box melody that plays during that sequence, "Memory," recurs in various guises in the series, usually on different instruments. A jazzy version becomes the series' most common final-scene music, right before the iconic "See you, space cowboy" message (or its multiple variations) and the ending credits. It reminds viewers of this scene, which remains unexplained until session 5, "Ballad of Fallen Angels."

This session begins as Mao Yenrai, a former associate of Spike's, becomes the latest bounty head. Spike is eager to go after him, as is Faye, but Jet has a bad feeling about it due to Spike's reaction. Jet knows that, despite trying to escape his past, Spike has an obsession, combined with disregard for his own safety, with settling debts from that past, particularly in his crusade against the aptly named Vicious and his search for his former lover, Julia.[2] When Jet conducts research on the bounty target, he realizes Mao is connected to Spike's past. By then, Faye has already left to pursue him, with a ticket to the opera as Mao's date. She finds him dead, murdered by Vicious, who confronts her. When Spike learns what has happened, he goes after Vicious, and in a key scene it becomes clear that Mao is not the only one who is haunting Spike.

This scene is the "Green Bird" sequence, one of the most celebrated musical sequences in the *Cowboy Bebop* series. Its unusual music has much to do with its fame. Watanabe cited it as a prime example of the way that he deliberately chooses music that defies expectations (Watanabe, interview). After a violent showdown with Vicious (18:51), Spike falls through the windows of a cathedral, seemingly (but not really) to his death, while his life flashes before his eyes. It's not a scene that would suggest the gentle chorus and piano melody, part lullaby and part hymn, that accompanies it. The calm music and violent visuals are audiovisual and counterpoint to each other.

The music features a chorus of high, childlike voices (all sung by Kanno) in a repeating melody alternating between homophonic style and canonic imitation. It is heard as Spike falls, and the first moments of his memory flash across the screen. As the piano accompaniment enters, scenes of Spike fighting with Vicious appear, followed by a mysterious blonde woman named Julia. This scene builds on the initial scene from session 1, with Spike walking in the rain and a fallen rose. It fleshes out the basics of the story: Spike and Vicious were once friends, working in a criminal organization, but a woman came between them, and when she and Spike attempted to leave, the consequences were violent (in one frame, a gun is pointed to Julia's head). While the details are articulated later in the "Jupiter Jazz" and "The Real Folk Blues" sessions, the "Green Bird" sequence begins to explain why Spike is so emotionally invested in fighting with Vicious. This narration is accomplished not with dialogue, but with only visuals and music.

How does the scene tell us so much without having the characters speak? The visuals show not only actions but also emotions: Spike and Vicious fight back-to-back, smiling at each other, with guns in their hands; Julia looks down at Spike in bed; or Julia stays still with a gun pointed to her head. In addition, the music suggests through the larger associations of its style, as well as those specific to the series. The instrumentation and childlike sound connect it to "Memory," and the visuals build off an earlier scene that used the music-box version of the cue. With the repeated use of "Memory" in other forms throughout the series, the viewer senses that "Green Bird" is a part of the mysterious larger narrative of Spike's story.

As with the music-box version of "Memory," the voices and repetitive musical style suggest a connection to childhood and nostalgia. The musical mood suggests that Spike looks back on this time with fondness, before everything violently fell apart. It so heavily occupies his memory that he will resort to anything—even his own death—to put it right. Still, as we see elsewhere in the series, Spike feels the need to maintain a certain façade and to adapt, to the point of getting angry at his crewmates when they remind him of his past. "Ballad of Fallen Angels" shows that he cannot fully adapt, and the music is the key to understanding this aspect of Spike's character.

These are my personal impressions of the role of music in that scene. However, Shinichirō Watanabe said that Spike was intended to be a fallen angel (hence the title of the session)—perhaps someone who retains an essential goodness, despite the wrongs and scars of his past. That scene makes the metaphorical literal: "Spike is falling. The scene has the double meaning of Spike as a fallen angel. So I fit it with angel-like music" (Watanabe, interview). He chose the hymn-like "Green Bird," in a way not foreseen or intended by Kanno.[3]

Cowboy Bebop is full of characters defined by their past, whether it's because they can't escape it (Spike), they're unable to acknowledge it at all (Faye), or somewhere in-between (Jet). They have all fallen from some innocence or grace, separated from their histories by irreconcilable circumstances. While all three have dark moments of no return in their pasts, they also retain the potential for a redemptive future.

"Rain" is another sequence, earlier in the session, where much of the meaning is conveyed through music. Watanabe said that he had not ordered the music for the "Rain" sequence as a vocal work; in fact, he had requested Kanno to produce only one vocal song for the entire series (for "a scene of Julia in the summertime"), but she produced more than ten vocal songs, including "Rain," out of sheer inspiration. To accommodate the song, Watanabe removed much of the dialogue for that scene: "The problem with vocal songs is that you usually have dialogue, and the lyrics of the songs cover them up, or the meanings don't really match. They're difficult to use. With 'Rain,' I decided to put in the song but take out the dialogue. I prioritized the music and made the scene fit it" (Watanabe, interview). As a result, most of the drama of the moment is conveyed through cryptic one-liners between Vicious and Spike.

Sung by Mai Yamane, "Rain" plays as Spike enters the cathedral where Vicious is holding Faye. Spike plans to confront him over killing Mao and other baggage from the past. The dialogue during this sequence reflects the fallen-angel themes that Watanabe has described. Vicious says to Spike as he enters, "When angels are forced out of heaven, they become devils. You agree, don't you, Spike?" Spike's answer belies the idea that the lyrics to "Rain" are that different from the dialogue, as he says, "I'm just watching a bad dream I never wake up from."

The lyrics of "Rain" include the line, "Wish this were a dream, but no, it isn't," and the message connects to themes in other episodes that suggest that Spike's life is but a dream. The words of the song also reinforce the fallen-angel concept, with lyrics like "Mother never danced through fire showers," and, "If there is a hell / I'm sure this is how it smells." The refrain, "Walk in the rain / Walk in the rain," references fighting through difficult circumstances, as "bad weather" often does in music. (In Spike's case, this lyric also references the rain in his flashback with Julia and the fallen rose.) The imagery in the lyrics connects to the idea of Spike being forced to walk through hell—just like a fallen angel, torn from heaven. The song's message is an interesting counterpoint to Vicious's dialogue, in which he goads Spike for not being as evil as he used to be. Mao, he says, had to die because "he was a beast who lost his fangs"; Spike must die for the same reason.

If music in "Ballad of Fallen Angels" helps to establish Spike's backstory, it does so for the supporting characters in the next two Spike-focused episodes, "Jupiter Jazz" Parts 1 and 2. These sessions reveal who Julia is and why she is so important to Spike. We also meet Gren, an episodic character who also knows Vicious. Music plays an even more direct role in establishing Gren's connection to Vicious and its continuing importance to him, which foreshadows Spike's fate.

Gren and Spike's Musical Memories

The "Jupiter Jazz" sessions are central to the arc about Spike, Vicious, and Julia. They include important revelations about Spike's past that help to set up the two "Real Folk Blues" sessions, which conclude the arc. However, "Jupiter Jazz" spends much of its runtime focused on other characters besides Spike, particularly Faye and her relationship with Gren, one of *Cowboy Bebop*'s strongest episodic characters.

Faye meets Gren at a bar on Callisto, where he is playing the saxophone. While she is taken by "Mr. Saxophone," he insists he's not interested in women. None the less, they manage to make a personal connection. When Faye is set upon by thugs, Gren rescues her and takes her to his place. There, he tells her about his past, including the tune that he played at the bar. Although he doesn't tell Faye about the music's connection to Vicious, she sees a picture of them together and hears Vicious's voice on the answering machine, asking Gren if he wants to meet. Suspicious, Faye confronts Gren in the shower, where she not only learns that he is intersex but also about his relationship with Vicious.

Gren had fought alongside Vicious in a war on Titan, a moon of Saturn. While crouching in a trench together, Gren heard Vicious listening to a music box, and Gren asked if he could play the melody on his saxophone. Vicious handed the music box to Gren and suddenly threw a knife near him. Initially alarmed, Gren realized that the knife was thrown at a scorpion that was about to attack him. This act helped Vicious to gain Gren's trust and led to their friendship during the war. Gren's sexuality and his attachment to his memory of Vicious suggest a homoerotic overlay, at least from Gren's end.

Gren is playing the tune from the music box on his saxophone when Faye meets him at the bar. Called "Space Lion," the song reverberates throughout the "Jupiter Jazz" sessions, both diegetically and non-diegetically. A leitmotiv for Gren, it represents his attachment to Vicious, or at least the person Gren once believed him to be.[4] This nostalgic attachment to the past, as well as the role of music in it, has parallels to Spike's story and its musical representation. The sessions juxtapose Gren's and Spike's stories when Vicious uses the code name "Julia" to lure Spike into a confrontation. Viewers also learn that Gren had met her once in the bar where he plays saxophone. Their stories connect in Gren's final moments, when he tells Spike how Julia seemed and that she was talking about him. This further clarifies the similarities between them—including the similar roles of music. In Gren's case, however, the relationship between music and memory is much more explicit. The music exists diegetically in his world, and he connects it to his memories: Vicious gave him the music box with the tune he loved, he learned to play it, and he still performs it regularly at the bar on Callisto.

Both Gren's and Spike's themes represent memories of an idealized past. Unlike Spike, Gren doesn't seem to have seen

Vicious since the war. Spike knows that the Vicious he knew (or thought he knew) no longer exists. However, Gren doesn't let go of his previous vision of Vicious; even as his war buddy shoots and mortally wounds him, Gren expresses a wish to go back to that past, asking Spike to route his ship to Titan. When Spike says he'll never survive all the way there (Callisto orbits Jupiter, while Titan orbits Saturn), he insists, saying it is fine if he dies on the way.

Gren at least recognizes Vicious's now sinister nature enough to try to damage him; he turns his music box into a bomb and throws it on Vicious's ship of red-eye (a popular illegal drug that shows up in many sessions of *Cowboy Bebop*, including the first one). However, he can't bring himself to destroy his old comrade. His death flying to Titan is symbolic of his story; Gren dies while trying to recreate a past that can never return, a longing for friendship with someone who may have always manipulated him. Spike accepts that the past is over, but he can't help trying to set things right whenever it catches up to him. Gren's absorption with his past and refusal to accept that it is over is represented by the diegetic nature of "Space Lion." Spike's "Memory" reminds the audience of how haunted he is by the past, but Spike makes it clear to his crew mates that he does not like to be reminded of it. In contrast, Gren embraces his past memory by keeping the music that indexes it alive in his current life, through the music box and the saxophone.

"Space Lion" ends with a long version of the theme, evolving beyond the saxophone solo into a longer, more stylistically varied piece with Afropop-like drumming and choral style. It plays over the entire final minutes of the session, including the end credits. According to Watanabe, this musical accompaniment was unprecedented in anime: "Usually anime has a part

A and a part B, each of which is ten minutes long. This episode has a seven-minute song at the end of part B ... it doesn't have dialogue in the last several minutes, which is all song. That's pretty radical in terms of making anime" (Watanabe, interview). As with "Ballad of Fallen Angels," Watanabe let the music lead the visuals: "I developed and edited the visuals so that the music fit perfectly ... and it would end in a way that felt good to watch" (Watanabe, interview). I agree with Watanabe that it fits perfectly, beyond matching visuals and sounds: The music expands outward from Gren's saxophone solo as if we're following Gren out to space, as we watch his space ship (and the *Bebop*) recede into the distance.

The placement of a long piece of music at the end of the session parallels the musical setting for the end of the series as a whole, in the second part of "The Real Folk Blues." The parallel draws further analogies between Gren's and Spike's stories, with the former foreshadowing the latter. But first, let us discuss the entirety of "The Real Folk Blues" and its music.

Spike's Story—and Music—Coming Full Circle

The title, "The Real Folk Blues," references Chess Records' 1960s compilations of its most famous blues artists, most notably the Muddy Waters album. Within the world of *Cowboy Bebop*, it also references the ending theme of most of the episodes, sung by Mai Yamane. It is one of the few vocal songs in the series that is in Japanese, with lyrics longing for a past or missing love. The music of this ending theme suggests a mournful jazz ballad, in a minor key, with heavy use of tenor saxophone in short solo bursts (like the lick that opens the song). It communicates a sense of longing and a nostalgic pathos.

While the video accompanying the opening theme "Tank!" features various cast members of *Cowboy Bebop*, the video for "The Real Folk Blues" addresses Spike's past, with the black-and-white shots of the shadowy alley and Julia featured in his flashbacks. At the beginning of the second stanza, the narrator speaks of watching the future with one eye and the past with the other; they recall Spike's line in these two episodes, in which Spike mentions seeing the present and the past. Spike feels as if he has no future; this episode, which ends with his death, proves him right. While "Tank!" represents the shiny, fun surface of the series, its cast of characters, and the bombastic action sequences, "The Real Folk Blues" reminds us of its emotional core, the story of Spike and Julia.

"The Real Folk Blues" finally gives context to the cryptic lyrics and images accompanying the ending theme. Part I begins as Julia learns that Vicious is attempting to take control of the Red Dragon syndicate, and that she is in danger. Later, Spike and Jet suffer an attempted assassination by the Red Dragons at their favorite bar; Spike learns where Julia is and goes to search for her. Faye finds Julia first, not realizing who she is until the end, when Julia insists that Faye tell Spike to meet her at "the place." A flashback reveals that "the place" is a graveyard where they had planned to meet after Spike left the syndicate. They meet there, but Julia points a gun at Spike (22:35), as Vicious has ordered her to kill him to save her own life. Here ends the first half of "The Real Folk Blues (Part 1)."

Musical themes weave through the memories of Spike and Julia. At the beginning of "The Real Folk Blues (Part 1)," "Memory" is reinterpreted as "Adieu," a cabaret ballad, revealing the familiar melody after an original introduction. The narrator's position is ambiguous, as she may be saying goodbye to a departing lover ("I stand alone / And watch you fade away like clouds / High up in the sky / I'm strong and so cold / As I stand alone / Goodbye, so long / Adieu"), or she may possibly be departing herself ("Don't care for me / Don't cry / Let's say goodbye, adieu / It's time to say goodbye / I know that in time / It will just fade away / It's time to say goodbye"). The singer also repeatedly sings, "Lost in a memory," but who or what is lost remains ambiguous: *she* may be lost in someone else's memory, or her lover may be lost in hers.

Like the song, "The Real Folk Blues" includes two goodbyes: Julia dies near the beginning of Part 2. She is shot when Vicious's crew catches up with them in the graveyard. Spike's life is also nearing its end, and he dies after killing Vicious at the conclusion of the session, marking the end of the series. The visuals remind the viewer of both of these characters: Part 1 opens with the rainy street presented in Spike's memory, followed by Julia, who hears the ominous warning, "The elders are making their move. Go quickly but quietly." The leaders of Red Dragon (the elders) retaliate against Vicious's attempted coup, and, as an associate of Vicious, Julia is also placed in danger. By extension, so is Spike, who is later attacked at the bar. Of course, this threat is just a red herring; it is Vicious, not the elders, who kills both Julia and Spike, leaving them as memories for each other and the other characters.

As a version of "Memory," "Adieu" connects this scene to Spike's memories while giving Julia agency. This scene marks the first appearance of Julia as herself, rather than filtered through Spike's black-and-white, rainy-day memories. In contrast to the simple music box of "Memory" (which the "Jupiter Jazz" sessions have already associated with fuzzy, faulty, idealized memories), "Adieu" has a human voice. The song could be interpreted as Julia singing, giving her voice to her part in the story, although the song also suggests the multiple perspectives of a dialogue, presumably with Spike.

Emily Bindiger's voice, heard in both "Adieu" and "Flying Teapot," connects the two main female protagonists in *Cowboy Bebop*. Faye and Julia are linked musically elsewhere, as in the end of "Ballad of Fallen Angels"; Julia's humming in Spike's dream turns out to be Faye's in real life. Faye and Julia actually meet in this episode, and their differences and similarities are made apparent. They're both beautiful women with attitude who know how to fend for themselves. But Julia is mysterious in her motives and apparent omniscience (automatically figuring out that Faye knows Spike), while Faye is more down-to-earth in her ignorance and flaws, including her awkwardness around a woman like Julia.

While these two sessions use fewer cues than others, they feature a few long musical moments that seem all the more significant. Toward the end of Part 1, Vicious takes over the syndicate, to "Road to the West." As this cue fades out, the original, music-box version of "Memory" fades in as Spike meets Julia in the graveyard. He picks up the rose from a grave, and she points a gun at Spike. A to-be-continued card covers the screen, and the music abruptly ends in the middle of a phrase. Their story is not yet over.

"Memory" is foregrounded at the beginning of Part 2, which starts without the opening theme; it is reprised as the episode intersperses flashbacks of their time in the syndicate as Spike and Julia catch up. She can't kill him, and collapses in his arms, wanting to leave with him. The spare texture of the music box forms an ironic contrast to the emotional heaviness of their dialogue, in which they give in to the weight of memories that bind them to each other over the imperative to live free. Vicious soon arrives and kills Julia; the absence of music and the slow-motion camera emphasize the shock of the moment.

Two other major musical moments in "The Real Folk Blues" are the session-title song and "Blue." A common tactic in anime is to use an ending theme or, more commonly, an opening theme for the climactic sequence in a final episode. In *Cowboy Bebop*, the final session carries the title of the ending theme. The melancholy feeling of this theme fits better with Spike's battle with the syndicate, rather than the more triumphant opening. Spike's suicidal mission to kill Vicious is another example of the way he chooses to be bound by his memories rather than being free of them. Spike triumphantly takes down the main villain but sadly succumbs to his own wounds. "Blue" plays immediately after Spike falls to the ground.

"Blue" begins with an a cappella choir of childlike voices, recalling "Green Bird." About forty-five seconds into the song it changes to a contemporary rock ballad, sung by Mai Yamane. As she sings, "Never seen a bluer sky," the camera pans up to the blue sky. The chorus declares, "Free / Wanna be free / gonna be free," suggesting that Spike is finally free in death. The initial choir is added quietly back into the texture as the chorus builds. Like "Space Lion," "Blue" is a relatively long song (five minutes) that plays through the credits, changing and combining genres. It is a visual and sonic callback to the end of "Jupiter Jazz," which suggests parallels in Gren's and Spike's fates.

Whether Spike dies at the end of the series is one of the most hotly debated aspects of the series, and one where Watanabe has usually been silent or vague in interviews, preferring for fans to make up their own minds. I have always taken the position that Spike dies, and the musical patterns across Spike's story and the foreshadowing provided by various songs point to his death. The music in Spike's five episodes suggests that Spike is doomed to succumb to the weight of his memories and draws strong parallels with the fates of other characters who die in related ways, such as Gren and Julia. Through several key, memorable musical moments, as well as the repeated placement and reworking of the "Memory" theme, the music of *Cowboy Bebop* gives Spike's short life story a poetic resonance, reinforcing its inevitable fate. This perception is confirmed by one last musical reference after the final credits of "The Real Folk Blues (Part 2)," where the message that usually reads "See you, space cowboy" says, instead, "You're gonna carry that weight"—a quote from *Abbey Road*, the last studio album the Beatles recorded before their breakup.[5] Just as the Beatles acknowledged that they'd carry the weight of their experience for a long time, the characters in *Bebop* can never fully escape the weight of their pasts—and none more so than Spike Spiegel.

Conclusion: You're Gonna Carry That Weight

The status of *Cowboy Bebop* as a mainstream, critically acclaimed, gateway anime grants it a far-reaching influence outside the medium, including upon major American directors like Quentin Tarantino. Not only does Tarantino share many of Watanabe's influences and fascinations (such as spaghetti westerns, blaxploitation, and John Woo; Fitzmaurice 2015), but he and his collaborators have also specifically cited *Bebop* as one of his influences. When Daryl Hannah asked Tarantino for films to watch that inspired the *Kill Bill* series, *Cowboy Bebop* was on the list (Downey 2004). Given the major role of music in the critical stature and popularity of *Cowboy Bebop*, a close study of its soundtrack sheds light on its impact on other music-conscious creators like Tarantino.

Another testament to *Cowboy Bebop*'s explosive popularity is the live performances of its music, featuring Kanno and her stable of musicians. Raj Ramayya said, "The first few shows, I was surprised by how many people were into this." Steve Conte said, "The crowd was *screaming*. It was like Beatlemania." Scott Matthew, who sang for the *Cowboy Bebop* movie and on Kanno's later soundtrack for *Ghost in the Shell: Stand Alone Complex*, described being chased by fans after one of his Tokyo concerts. These are powerful testaments to the emotional power of the work and the impact that it had on their careers. They were all very grateful for their experiences of working with Kanno. The musicians and actors clearly enjoyed the music, and it still had a powerful effect on them. Steve Blum, the English voice of Spike, told me that he "never had that emotional connection to music in a cartoon before, or since … I listen to the soundtrack all the time."

While I focused on the two scores most important to understanding *Cowboy Bebop* for the purposes of this short guide, Yōko Kanno's extensive career deserves a thorough-going study. This is especially true for her scores for *Ghost in the Shell: Stand Alone Complex* and *Terror in Resonance*. A wider survey of her work would include the *Macross* series (which first earned her fame in Japan), *The Vision of Escaflowne*, and *Turn A Gundam*. The score of *Terror in Resonance* would be especially fascinating to study, given its stylistic and thematic differences from previous Watanabe–Kanno collaborations.

The intricacies of the music of *Cowboy Bebop* are testimony to the worthiness of anime music as an object of analysis. This is especially true for directors like Watanabe, who are so closely attuned to the role of music, and fan-favorite composers like Kanno. I hope that in reading this book, readers are encouraged to explore their work beyond *Cowboy Bebop*, as well as that of other directors and composers who do innovative work with music. I hope this gateway anime becomes a gateway to the medium's many intriguing soundtracks.

Notes

1: The Work Which Becomes a Genre Itself

1. For more on Shibuya-*kei*, see the discussion of Ed and Ein's musical themes in Chapter 6.
2. This information comes from Watanabe's comments in the interview with series editor Noriko Manabe.
3. *Chanbara* is the Japanese term for the samurai film genre, explained further in Ahn (2013).
4. The Japanese policy of *sakoku* ("closed country"), enacted under the Tokugawa shogunate, officially prohibited all Westerners from entering or trading with Japan (with the exception of the Dutch), and Japanese nationals from leaving the country. The last of the edicts was enacted in 1639. This period of isolationism lasted over two centuries, its erosion beginning in 1854, with Commodore Matthew Perry's signing of the Convention of Kanagawa, which forced Japan to agree to trade relations with the U.S.
5. For more information on the musical choices for *Samurai Champloo*, see this February 8, 2006 interview with Shinichirō Watanabe at the Detroit Film Theater, http://www.spookhouse.net/angelynx/comics/watanabe-at-DIA.html (accessed July 16, 2016).
6. In *Blue Nippon* (2001), E. Taylor Atkins discusses the popularity of Art Blakey, among other American jazz musicians, in 1960s Japan.
7. Negative continuity refers to a lack of consistency among

characters and plots between episodes; for example, someone who dies in the previous episode can come back alive and well in the next one, or characters don't remember previous episodes' events. This is very common in Western animation series, especially gag comedies, short-based series (e.g., classic *Looney Tunes*, *Animaniacs*), or series aimed at children. In anime, however, this is relatively uncommon, as the storylines tend to be serialized. Adult Swim is a late-night bloc on Cartoon Network that plays cartoons aimed at older teens and adults, such as *Futurama*, *Family Guy*, and so on. It used to have an anime bloc of more violent, sexual, or darker series considered more appropriate for the Adult Swim audience; Watanabe's series like *Bebop* and *Champloo* were included in this programming bloc, which played a major role in their popularity in North America. The anime segment has since become its own Saturday night bloc, named after its 1990s/early 2000s daytime anime segment Toonami. This is where *Space Dandy* first aired in 2014, dubbed in English at the same time that it was airing in Japanese in Japan.

8 Masaki Yuasa is the director of the anime *Kaiba* (2008), *The Tatami Galaxy* (2010), and *Ping Pong* (2014), among other works. He has a very distinctive visual style, a huge departure from more typical anime art design, which has earned him a strong cult following around the world.

9 Sayo Yamamoto is now best known for directing the hit figure skating anime *Yuri!!! on Ice* (2016).

2: Mish-Mash Blues

1 Eclecticism is also a common Japanese cultural ideal that is an aspiration for many Japanese artists. See Manabe (2013).

2 Original video anime is a straight-to-video release.

3 For more information on the idol phenomenon, see Aoyagi (2005) and Stevens (2004, 2008).

4 Luke Plunkett, "The Banned Pokémon Episode that Gave Children Seizures," *Kotaku*, February 11, 2011, https://www.kotaku.com.au/2011/02/the-banned-pokemon-episode-that-gave-children-seizures/ (accessed April 11, 2017).

3: "Black Dog" Serenade

1 Led Zeppelin often attempted to hide their compositions' debts to the blues, such as with Howlin' Wolf's famous plagiarism case against them over "The Lemon Song." For further information on this, see Segrest and Hoffman (2005) and Headlam (1995). For more detailed studies of blues-rock, race, and authenticity, see Daley (2003) and Rudinow (1994).

2 E. Taylor Atkins (2001) discusses the issue of authenticity in Japanese jazz throughout *Blue Nippon*. For a broader look at the history of Japanese popular music (beyond jazz) in the mid-to-late twentieth century, including its relationship with Western music, see Michael K. Bourdaughs (2012).

3 "Rain" is sung by Mai Yamane in its use in session 5, "Ballad of Fallen Angels," but by Conte on the soundtrack release. The Yamane version is available on the movie soundtrack release, *COWBOY BEBOP O.S.T. FUTURE BLUES.*

4 For broader discussion on discourses of authenticity in popular and world music, see Taylor (1997).

5 Some notable writings on this subject include Herzog (2009) and chapter 6, "Narrative vs. Spectacle in the Hollywood Blockbuster," from King (2002). The author also took the course, "Action Film and the Soundtrack," with James Buhler

at the University of Texas at Austin in Fall 2015, with Hannah Lewis as a guest lecturer on similarities between action and musical sequences.

4: "Jupiter Jazz"

1 Moments when these colors are particularly vibrant include 7:37, during Spike's fight, and 12:47, as Spike is talking to Stella.

2 *Mise en scène* is a film studies term that refers to the overall visual composition of a scene.

3 Tongpu's name is also a reference to a song by Yellow Magic Orchestra, "Tong-Poo," from the same 1978 eponymous album that includes "Mad Pierrot."

5: "See You, Space Cowboy"

1 The "revisionist westerns" that emerged in the 1960s complicated the moral landscape of classic Hollywood westerns. The revisionist westerns favored grayer, more questionable moral landscapes and darker settings with more realistic violence, compared with the classic westerns. These (anti)heroes had less honorable motives and were more willing to resort to harming innocent people compared to heroes of classic westerns.

2 For more information on the music of *Animaniacs*, see Scoggin (2016).

3 Comments include "Absoultely inspired by Ennio Morricone!" by user Nick D'Orazio, "clint eastwood?? xD" by user Juancho Barahona, and most tellingly, from user Big Slammo: "I actually thought this was from a Sergio Leone film when I first heard it all those years ago." videgenial2, "Cowboy Bebop OST 3 Blue – Go Go Cactus Man," YouTube video, duration 2:37, posted August 25, 2008. https://www.youtube.com/watch?v=OaKH9bywzgQ&ab_channel=videgenial2 (accessed May 29, 2016). This is an unauthorized upload of the music. The author does not endorse this practice, but is simply documenting it as an example of online fan dialogue.

4 The Aeolian mode is the natural minor scale, equivalent to the notes A B C E D F G A. The Dorian mode is equivalent to D E F G A B C D.

5 A leitmotiv is a repeated musical theme, particularly an instrumental one, which recurs throughout narrative media to represent a specific character, object or idea. It has its roots in Richard Wagner's music dramas such as the *Ring* Cycle, before being widely adopted in film scoring. I use this term to describe Andy's and Gren's themes but not those of the major *Cowboy Bebop* characters, as the main characters' themes are full songs (rather than just motifs) and play more complicated narrative roles. See also Chapters 6 and 7.

6 By "episodic characters," I mean characters who only appear in this one particular episode, rather than major or supporting cast members such as Spike, Faye, Vicious, etc., who recur throughout the show. The characters in "Mushroom Samba" who represent blaxploitation actors and character types do not appear in any other episodes.

7 Terms like "characters of color" or "non-white characters" are problematic in the sense that Americans consider Asians to be non-white, while anime like *Cowboy Bebop* originate from Japan. In most anime, main characters, including Japanese ones, are depicted as fair-skinned; some, like Sailor Moon, may be written as Japanese but have blonde hair and blue eyes. Hence it is not always clear whether a character is Caucasian or Japanese from the way the character is drawn. The races of the main characters in *Cowboy Bebop* are difficult to determine, especially given the racially and culturally diverse backdrop of *Cowboy Bebop*'s world. On the other hand, some anime depict non-Japanese, non-white characters with exaggerated facial features rather than hair, eye, or skin color alone. These features make the racial identities of episodic or background characters easier to identify. The black characters in "Mushroom Samba" are similarly easily identified.

8 *Super Fly*, the film title, is two separate words, while "Superfly," the song, is spelled as one word.

6: Jamming with Edward (and Jet and Faye)

1 Fanservice is defined in the *Anime News Network* Encyclopedia as elements or moments injected into an anime purely to please fans, "with no direct relevance to the story or character development." The most common use of the term, and the one I am using, refers to sexualized character designs, typically "scantily clothed, seductively posed, well-endowed women." See "Fan service," Lexicon, ANN Encyclopedia, *Anime News Network*, http://www.animenewsnetwork.com/encyclopedia/lexicon.php?id=54 (accessed December 29, 2015).

2 "Flying Teapot" vocalist Emily Bindiger told me that the lyric was originally "Uranus." She suggested that the choice was not good for English-speaking listeners and that the songwriters should change it to "Venus."

7: "Ballad of Fallen Angels"

1 This is a reference to Milan Kundera's novel, *The Unbearable Lightness of Being* (2005 [1984]), about four people living in the shadow of the 1968 Prague Spring uprising in Czechoslovakia. One of the primary themes is that a life without the ties of relationships and goals, or a lighter life, is actually more difficult than a heavier one, and that the heavier one is more worth living. Analyzing Spike's journey, particularly his attempt to run from the ties of his past, only to be swept back into them, reminded me of this novel.

2 These names could also be musical references. Vicious could possibly refer to the Sex Pistols' bassist Sid Vicious, and Julia to John Lennon's mother, who was the inspiration for the eponymous song on the Beatles' White Album (*The Beatles*, 1968). This reading also fits with Julia's role in the series as a phantasm of Spike's past, given the similarly haunted way in which John Lennon wrote about his late mother in his music.

3 Watanabe did not order "Green Bird." Kanno had composed it out of inspiration, thinking it could fit a pretty scene. It was Watanabe's idea to use it to accompany an attempted murder.

4 As noted in Chapter 5, Note 5, I am using the term leitmotiv to describe Gren's theme but not those of the major *Cowboy Bebop* characters, which are full songs rather than motives. The saxophone melody from "Space Lion" is used specifically to represent Gren's presence and is heard as a brief motive until the end of the episode.

5 Although *Abbey Road* was released before *Let it Be* (in September 1969 vs. May 1970), the recording sessions for *Abbey Road* took place after those for *Let it Be*.

Bibliography

Abrams, Simon. "*Cowboy Bebop*: Heavy Metal Queen." *The A.V. Club*. July 23, 2011. Available online: http://www.avclub.com/tvclub/cowboy-bebop-heavy-metal-queen-59205 (accessed July 4, 2016).

Ahn, Jiwon. "Samurai Champloo: Transnational Viewing." In *How to Watch Television*, eds. Ethan Thompson and Jason Mittell, 364–72. New York: New York University Press, 2013.

Aoyagi, Hiroshi. *Island of Eight Million Smiles: Idol Performance and Symbolic Production in Contemporary Japan*. Cambridge, MA: Harvard University Press, 2005.

Atkins, E. Taylor. *Blue Nippon: Authenticating Jazz in Japan*. Durham, NC: Duke University Press, 2001.

Bourdaughs, Michael K. *Sayonara Amerika, Sayonara Nippon: A Geopolitical Prehistory of J-Pop*. New York: Columbia University Press, 2012.

Daley, Mike. "'Why Do Whites Sing Black?': The Blues, Whiteness and Early Histories of Rock." *Popular Music and Society* 26 (2) (2003): 161–7.

Downey, Ryan J. "What Made 'Bill' Kill: Quentin's Blood-Spattered Rundown." *MTV News*, June 10, 2004. Available online: http://www.mtv.com/news/1488333/what-made-bill-kill-quentins-blood-spattered-rundown/ (accessed November 28, 2016).

Dyer, Richard. "Music and Presence in Blaxploitation Cinema." In *In the Space of a Song: The Uses of Song in Film*, 156–74. New York: Routledge, 2013.

Fitzmaurice, Larry. "Quentin Tarantino: The Complete Syllabus of His Influences and References." *Slate*. September 1, 2015. Available online: http://www.slate.com/blogs/browbeat/2015/09/01/quentin_tarantino_influences_and_references_every_inspiration_for_pulp_fiction.html (accessed November 28, 2016).

Gorbman, Claudia. *Unheard Melodies: Narrative Film Music*. Bloomington: Indiana University Press, 1987.

Headlam, Dave. "Does the Song Remain the Same?: Questions of Authorship and Identification in the Music of Led Zeppelin." In *Concert Music, Rock, and Jazz Since 1945: Essays and Analytical Studies*, eds. Elizabeth West Marvin and Richard Hermann, 313–63. Rochester: University of Rochester Press, 1995.

Herzog, Amy. *Dreams of Difference, Songs of the Same: The Musical Moment in Film*. Minneapolis: University of Minnesota Press, 2009.

King, Geoff. *New Hollywood Cinema: An Introduction*. New York: Columbia University Press, 2002.

Kundera, Milan. *The Unbearable Lightness of Being*. New York: Harper Perennial, 2005. Original English edition published by Harper & Row, 1984.

Leinberger, Charles. *Ennio Morricone's* The Good, the Bad and the Ugly*: A Film Score Guide*. Lanham, MD: Scarecrow Press, 2004.

Leinberger, Charles. "The Dollars Trilogy: 'There Are Two Kinds of Western Heroes, My Friend!'" In *Music in the Western: Notes from the Frontier*, ed. Kathryn Kalinak, 131–47. New York: Routledge, 2012.

Manabe, Noriko. "Representing Japan: 'National' Style among Japanese Hip-Hop DJs." *Popular Music* 32 (1) (January 2013): 35–50.

Manabe, Noriko. *The Revolution Will Not Be Televised: Protest Music After Fukushima*. New York: Oxford University Press, 2015.

Roberts, Martin. "'A New Stereophonic Sound Spectacular': Shibuya-kei as Transnational Soundscape." *Popular Music* 32 (1) (January 2013): 111–23.

Rose, Tricia. "Flow, Layering, and Rupture in Postindustrial New York" (1994). Reprinted in *Signifyin(g), Sanctifyin' and Slam Dunking: A Reader in African American Expressive Culture*, ed. Gena Dagel Caponi, 191–221. Amherst: University of Massachusetts Press, 1999.

Rudinow, Joel. "Race, Ethnicity, Expressive Authenticity: Can White People Sing the Blues?" *Journal of Aesthetics and Art Criticism* 52 (1) (1994): 127–37.
Scoggin, Lisa. *The Music of* Animaniacs*: Postmodern Nostalgia in a Cartoon World*. Hillsdale, NY: Pendragon Press, 2016.
Segrest, James and Mark Hoffman. *Moanin' at Midnight: The Life and Times of Howlin' Wolf*. New York: Thunder's Mouth Press, 2005.
Stevens, Carolyn. "Buying Intimacy: Proximity and Exchange at a Japanese Rock Concert." In *Fanning the Flames: Fans and Consumer Culture in Contemporary Japan*, ed. William W. Kelly, 59–78. Albany: State University of New York Press, 2004.
Stevens, Carolyn. *Japanese Popular Music: Culture, Authenticity and Power*. New York: Routledge, 2008.
Stilwell, Robynn J. "The Fantastical Gap Between Diegetic and Non-Diegetic." In *Beyond the Soundtrack*, eds Daniel Goldmark, Lawrence Kramer, and Richard Leppert, 184–202. Berkeley: University of California Press, 2007.
Takahashi, Osamu. "Kanno Yōko Long Interview." *Music Magazine* 41/8/554 (July 2009), 45–7.
Tasker, Yvonne. *The Hollywood Action and Adventure Film*. Chichester: John Wiley & Sons, 2015.
Taylor, Timothy D. *Global Pop: World Music, World Markets*. New York: Routledge, 1997.
Tomita, Akihiro. "Interview: Anime Soundtracker Yōko Kanno." *Red Bull Music Academy*. November 2014. http://daily.redbullmusicacademy.com/2014/11/yoko-kanno-interview (accessed July 12, 2016).

Interviews

Bindiger, Emily. Skype interview with the author. May 31, 2016.

Blum, Steve, and Mary McGlynn. Skype interview with the author. July 19, 2016.

Conte, Steve. Skype interview with the author. May 10, 2016.

Kanno, Yōko. Email exchange with Noriko Manabe, with questions from the author. December 4, 2016.

Matthew, Scott. Skype interview with the author. June 21, 2016.

Ramayya, Raj. Skype interview with the author. April 29, 2016.

Watanabe, Shinichirō, and Yukiko Kiba. Interview by Noriko Manabe. Tokyo, July 8, 2016.

Index

CPSIA information can be obtained
at www.ICGtesting.com
Printed in the USA
LVHW012021290319
612339LV00014B/195/P